D1369100

BI
1.3.34
a.c

SVEN-GÖRAN ERIKSSON

The Inner Game – Improving Performance

ON FOOTBALL

With Willi Railo
& Håkan Matson

WITHDRAWN

Evesham & Malvern Hills College
Library

27810

WARWICKSHIRE COLLEGE
LIBRARY

Class No:
796.334 ERI

Acc No:
27810   SL

This is a Carlton Book

Text © Sven-Göran Eriksson, Willi Railo & Håkan Matson 2000
English text © MNR International B.V. & ITS Translations Ltd 2001
Design © Carlton Books Limited 2002

This edition published 2003

1 3 5 7 9 10 8 6 4 2

This book is sold subject to the condition that it shall not, by way of trade or
otherwise, be lent, resold, hired out or otherwise circulated without the
publisher's prior written consent in any form of cover or binding other than that
in which it is published and without a similar condition, including this condition,
being imposed upon the subsequent purchaser.

All rights reserved.

A CIP catalogue for this book is available from the British Library.

ISBN 1 84442 773 0

Executive Editor: Vanessa Daubney
Project Art Direction: Mark Lloyd
Design: Vaseem Bhatti
Jacket Design: Steve Lynn
Picture Research: Debora Fioravanti
Production: Sarah Corteel

Printed and bound in Great Britain

SVEN-GÖRAN ERIKSSON

The Inner Game – Improving Performance

ON FOOTBALL

With Willi Railo
& Håkan Matson

EVESHAM COLLEGE
LIBRARY

| CLASS NUMBER | 796.334 |
| ACCESSION NUMBER | 27810 |

CARLTON
BOOKS

Praise for On Football and Sven-Göran Eriksson:

Eriksson conjures revolution in the mind

The Guardian

'These guys know what they're doing... This book will challenge the way you look at sport but perhaps moore crucially, it will leave you assured that the England team is in safe hands.'

Four Four Two

'Eriksson is toast of two nations'

The Daily Telegraph

'An expert insider's theories as to what makes a sportsman tick... I thought it was excellent

Free Kick

'The thoughts of Eriksson ... and trusted sports psychologist, Willi Railo, on the mental side of the game... For players wishing to be part of his set-up, it is required reading.'

The Observer

'As his exhaustive research into the sporting mind shows, Eriksson is well-prepared.'

Sunday People

Contents

Foreword

Since this book was written, big things have happened to Sven-Göran Eriksson. In January 2001, he was appointed as manager of the England national team and a number of doubts were raised about the choice of a non-Englishman. Sven-Göran Eriksson himself, though, never had any doubts about accepting the assignment, as he says:

'This is the biggest job ever offered to me. My intention had been to stay another year with Lazio in Rome, but when the offer from the FA came, I immediately felt, "This is exactly what I want to do. Such an offer comes only once in a lifetime." It was too good to decline.

'Before accepting the position, I never made an analysis of the risks involved. I never thought, "I won't succeed." On the contrary, I thought, "If I don't accept, I won't be able to sleep at night, just ponder what I could have done with the job."

'My intuition told me what to do, as it has done so every time a new offer has come up – from the day when I took on IFK Gothenburg in the 1970s. Of course, it is a big change to take on England, but for me it was a larger step and even a greater risk to move from the little village of Torsby with the coaching job of the third Division team of Degerfors to the big and mighty IFK Gothenburg, one of the greatest football teams in Sweden. In fact, the step from Rome to London doesn't feel so big to me.

'I don't give much thought to being a foreigner. Sweden had an English coach (George Raynor) in 1958 and went to the World Cup finals. Why, then, shouldn't a Swede go to England? I have read the book *The Second Most Important Job in the Country*, which is all about the England coaches from 1949 through to Kevin Keegan. It shows that all of them have been declared idiots at some time in their career, even Sir Alf Ramsey, who took England to gold medals in the 1966 World Cup.

'So, I know what to expect. I didn't take the job for the money and not for the weather, either! I took it because it's England.'

Sven-Göran Eriksson
April 2001

Introduction

You miss in critical situations and you dare not take the initiative. You're at your best in training and never when it really matters. You flee when you should fight and become defensive when you should go on the offensive. You're afraid of losing, but just as afraid of winning.

Improving performance from within is crucial and this book deals with how you can use your mental powers to put your resources to better use. Naturally, the book focuses on football, but with its mixture of theory and practical examples, it describes how your inner side can be decisive, not only in football, but also in many other areas outside sport.

Beginning with the inspirational tale of how Sven-Göran Eriksson took the Italian club Lazio to their first League win in 26 years, the authors examine how good sportsmen and women must develop an outlook which gives them the power not only to believe that they can win, but also to accept that if they should not, it is just a stepping stone towards that goal.

Elsewhere, they look at how to go about creating a strong feeling of self-confidence, coping with pressure, and setting goals, i.e. achievable targets, which will in turn lead to those ultimate goals. And, with an all important chapter on developing a winning culture within a team and the role of the coach in creating that culture, the book culminates with advice on how to change negative thoughts into positive ones.

Anyone interested in football cannot fail to be aware of Sven-Göran Eriksson and his appointment as manager of the England team in January 2001. His credentials for the post speak for themselves, since he has enjoyed a long and successful career as a football coach, training some of Europe's top teams to be winners instead of losers – from his first triumph with IFK Gothenburg in Sweden in winning the UEFA Cup in 1982, to wins in Portugal and Europe with Benfica and Roma, Sampdoria and of course, Lazio, in Italy. His wealth of experience is evident as he explains his philosophy on building winning teams.

Doctor Willi Railo, with his psychological techniques, has trained many sportsmen and women on their way to winning world championships and Olympic gold medals. He has written several books about performance and psychology, in sport as well as in management.

They have been helped on this project by the journalist Håkan Matson, who reported on Sven-Göran Eriksson's first European success and who has assisted Willi Railo with previous publications.

As the authors say, this book is the beginning of a pilgrimage, one which can lead to better performance, not just in football or any other sport, but in every aspect of one's life.

LO SCUDETTO

– Winning the Italian League

We sometimes say that nothing is impossible. But much more often we accept that it really is impossible to do certain things, to reach certain goals, to succeed with something we have set our minds on. Everyone said that it was impossible for Lazio to win the Italian League on 19 March 2000. The team had just lost to Verona 0–1 and all the experts and journalists were sure that the curtain had now come down: Lazio had once again missed *Lo Scudetto*. Even the club's owner had given up. 'When we lost in Verona and were nine points behind Juventus, I reckoned it was all over,' said Sergio Cragnotti.

Just two months later, the celebrations in the Olympic Stadium were unimaginable. Overjoyed fans surged onto the pitch trying to tear the clothes off the players – and succeeded in a couple of cases, too. Lazio had won the league. The impossible had become reality.

How did it happen? Naturally, a number of different factors came into it, but one thing is certain beyond all doubt: without the right mental attitude, Lazio's victory would never have been possible. *Lo Scudetto* was not won just with the feet. It was won at least as much with the power of the mind.

It is with this inner power that this book will be dealing.

Let's begin by letting Sven-Göran Eriksson himself describe the turning-point in Lazio's history – from nine points behind Juventus on 19 March to victory in the League on 14 May.

Sven-Göran Eriksson: 'In critical situations, you have to continue to motivate your players, to calm things down, while you explain that there still is a chance of winning.

'It was also extremely important to spend extra time talking to my most important players, the ones that could take the whole team with them. In pressure situations, you have to expect the younger players to hang back, reacting through fear and simple cowardice. As coach, you can't put too much pressure on them.

'The turning point came against Chelsea in the Champions' League on 22 March. We had to win to get into the quarter-finals. I thought to myself, if we lose, I'll have to settle for seeing out the season with Lazio – and then getting the boot. But on the outside I didn't give the game away. I knew that the lads were playing with a knife at their throats and were under a lot of mental pressure. But their problems were only in their heads, not their legs. If only we could get our concentration back, I knew we would be capable of beating any one.

'After the first half, things looked pretty bleak. We were trailing 0–1, but even so we didn't lose our belief and morale. The team showed character, the players really wanted to fight – and in the end we won 2–1. Then we won the derby against Roma (2–1) and the away match against the league leaders Juventus (1–0), and suddenly everything had changed.

'I often used to say that I could tell beforehand in the changing room if the team was ready. I noticed it especially when we got together after our warm-up. Everyone was in an attacking frame of mind, everyone believed in himself. It felt like the changing room was going to explode. Of course, this was no guarantee that you'd win but it was a guarantee that everybody was really committed to winning. What is decisive in critical situations is the atmosphere in the squad.

'A good atmosphere is not something that can be built up in a short time. It takes work and patience. I always tried to instil a "we" feeling amongst all the players. I believe the mental attitude is even more important during the final stages of a season, for then it's too late to change your tactics and technique.

'So little is required to be successful in sport. It's certainly mostly a matter of psychology, and in the end it's that psychological difference that decides whether you win or lose.

And of course, you've got to have a little luck. Then the impossible can become reality… at last.'

PERFORMANCE

– Daring to win

France '98: The football World Cup. The whole world was expecting Brazil's Ronaldo to step forward as the tournament's king, particularly after his fantastic performances in the Italian League. But the world was to see a shadow of the real Ronaldo. He was well below par in several matches, and quite woeful in the World Cup final against France. How could this happen?

Eriksson:

Of course, I don't know the inside story of the World Cup, but what often happens in similar cases is that there is anxiety over performance. The pressure's too great. Almost every day, I see players who are very good in training, but who are poor in match situations. Often, I see players who dominate in ordinary league matches but who practically disappear from the scene in an important cup match or a final.

Willi Railo:

How does anxiety about a performance affect a player?

Eriksson:

It can show itself in many ways. For instance, when I've called in players suffering from performance anxiety, they often take it so hard that they start to cry as they leave the pitch. When I talk to them in peace and quiet after the match, they say: 'I'm desperate to do well but at the same time I'm scared stiff of making mistakes and losing. That would be a disaster...' So I'm normally very careful about calling in players who happen to have had a bad day. But sometimes the team's performance has to come before any consideration of an individual player.

> I want to win so much that I lose

Some grow into the job

Railo:

I have worked with athletes in most sports and have seen how many of them also react in the opposite way – they turn an emergency into a positive force. No doubt you've had the same sort of experience?

Eriksson:

Absolutely. I've had many players who grew into the job, who were best when the chips were down. Mihajlovic, whom I had at Lazio for several years, always wants to win everything – even in goal-shooting practice. He doesn't believe that he can lose, and even if he does, it makes no impression on him. In every match he plays with exactly the same attitude: he's going to win. Christian Vieri is another such player. He has enormously high ambitions but doesn't worry if something goes wrong. He always maintains the same high level and is not afraid of doing what he wants, regardless of how the match is going. And when the match is over – well, then it's over. When the final whistle goes, Vieri won't waste energy blaming himself or senselessly looking for errors. I must also mention Veron, another one with the mental qualities that allowed him to grow into the job. When others tend to be defensive, his offensive thinking can be infectious.

In general, I would say that you need a core of three players with these qualities in a team, as it's natural for many players to become hesitant and defensive if the team suffers a setback. Your core group then has to function as a counterweight to stabilise the team.

Railo:

There are three factors, apart from physique, that will determine how well we do:

- Ideas.
- Emotions.
- Mental energy.

Earlier, we gave examples of how mental factors can be important in one's ability to perform, both where the team and the individual are concerned. We will be giving many more examples of this throughout the book.

There is a whole range of emotions which can influence performance, whether curbing or stimulating it, and in this respect there are many psychological elements that will affect performance, whether positively or negatively.

Can you, on the basis of your experience, name the most important factor in achieving success?

Eriksson:

I would say, most definitely, self-confidence. When two teams are equally strong in technique, tactics and feel for the game, the team with the greater self-confidence is going to win.

> No self-confidence – no success

Natural winners

Railo:

True, that goes for all sports. Let me take an example from another sport.

> Alberto Tomba – a natural winner

The skier, Alberto Tomba, always competed with great self-confidence. Unlike his opponents, he had the mental strength to win and win and win again, even after setbacks. A Norwegian skier did defeat Tomba in the 1992 Olympics. But these were his words after the competition:

'The difference between me and Tomba is that he sees himself as a natural winner.

Even if he loses, he still sees himself as a natural winner. I know that I am capable of winning – but for me, it isn't "natural" to win as much and so often as Tomba.

'I'm just as good as Tomba, physically and technically, and can beat him now and again, as I did in the Olympics. But there's still a difference between Tomba and me – and it's on the mental level.'

Eriksson:

Some athletes have this wonderful ability always to win. It's as though it's a natural state of mind for them.

Railo:

That's exactly what it is. Real winners not only know that they can win – many sportsmen know this – they have also fully accepted themselves as winners. It may sound strange to say this, but they dare to win, where others dare neither to win nor to lose.

Eriksson:

Looking at my own sport, football, I know that the mental situation in an instant of play will almost completely determine how the players and the team can utilise their ability. Concentration, motivation, self-confidence and team spirit directly affect performance.

The ability to make the right decision – and then dare to do the right thing in all situations – is decisive at the top of the modern game. If one player isn't up for it mentally, the whole team can collapse. My most recent experience of how important our mental processes can be is provided by Lazio. We had had a string of good matches and won many of them – but suddenly we lost 5–2 to Valencia. Psychology does count.

Railo:

Do you think it's always the most talented players in football who are the winners in the end?

Eriksson:

Unfortunately, no. Talent is only a prerequisite for success. If you look at the top footballers, playing ability among many of them is very even. We can't train more than we do, either. We're already at the maximum that players can take nowadays. So it's mental differences which will decide who the real winners are.

> Mental differences decide who the winners are

Railo:

I believe that nearly all practitioners of sports erect barriers which stop them from utilising their ability to the full. They allow their own minds to block performance. I once worked with a top-class Italian player. We went through different play situations and I asked him to close his eyes and to create mental images of his game. Everything went fine – until he had to think about Milan. Then he had a block. The reason was that this player had admired and looked up to Milan when he was a boy. So now, when he was in a position where he had to face his favourite team, his subconscious couldn't accept beating Milan.

Eriksson:

Before my time at the club, Lazio often used to lose against certain teams, in spite of the fact that Lazio were really much the better team. The only possible explanation was that the players in the team had a mental block, that psychologically and subconsciously they had accepted a defeat despite appearing outwardly confident of ending their losing streak.

I once had a world-class player who began to have problems finishing. He was fine away from the goal but seemed to be paralysed as soon as he entered the opponents' penalty area. He was hesitant and was never able to make use of a good position, making simple passes to team-mates instead. I didn't see this at all in training.

> ## Great in training – poor in important matches

It was the same story with a player who in training could take the most fantastic corners. In matches he always put them too near the goal, where they were gifts for the goalkeeper. I have had players who in training put away 99 per cent of their penalties, but in matches could only make 60 per cent of them. Others are active, attacking and constantly winning the ball – but only in training. In matches they just stand and stare.

Again, I have had players who were impossible to go past in training. They were good in matches, too – until the opponents had names like Ronaldo, Rivaldo or Vieri, who would practically be given free passage.

I have also made an analysis of the shooting of certain players. In ordinary games, 80 per cent went in. In the big matches, 80 per cent went wide of the mark.

I can only think that they must have had mental blocks which interfered with their ability to shoot at goal as often in one match as in another.

> ## A Manchester United player with a mental block

Railo:

I once worked with a player from Manchester United who had developed a mental block about scoring goals. I asked him to close his eyes and imagine himself in situations where he went into the penalty area, came up against the goalkeeper and shot the ball into the goal. He closed his eyes and imagined himself in this situation.

After a while I asked him, how did it go? He told me the ball went wide of the goal. We did this exercise seven more times, but with the same result: the ball went wide every time. Finally, I took over and said: 'I'll take the responsibility. You just go and score the goals.' I asked him how it had gone this time. He told me the ball went in. But when I asked him how it had felt, he said: 'I felt anxious, and had a headache.' This is just one example where, in order to be the best when it counts, we have to accept ourselves completely as winners, intellectually, emotionally, consciously and subconsciously. We have to use our mental energy to step on the accelerator, not to put the brakes on; but then we have to be able to handle the forces that pull us in different directions.

The will to win versus the fear of losing

You see, when we have to give a performance – a competition, a match, some task at work – there are two forces inside us pulling in different directions. One is 'ambition'. This is a positive force. Our ambition wants us to improve, to succeed, to attain the goals we have set ourselves, to win.

The other force is 'performance anxiety'. This is a negative force. It produces a fear of failing, of making mistakes, of disgracing ourselves and as a result, of not being accepted by others. These others might be our trainer, our team-mates, the media, supporters – and, in everyday life, friends, neighbours and workmates.

It is typical of players with high performance anxiety that they will 'punish' themselves when they make a mistake. This inner battle can be regarded as a tug-of-war – the strength of our ambition against our performance anxiety – that will determine the degree to which we will succeed. If our performance anxiety is too great, it won't matter that we have great ambition.

Railo:

One of Sweden's best football players of all time, Torbjörn Nilsson, was already a very good player in the Swedish League as a 20-year-old. He loved to play, he felt secure in his environment, and made the most of his talent. He obtained a professional contract with PSV Eindhoven when he was 22, and almost immediately things started to go wrong. And once these things began to happen, it got worse and Torbjörn was soon playing with half of his ability.

He returned to Sweden with high performance anxiety and his self-confidence gone. He soon began to play again, but not nearly as well as before he had set out on his adventure as a professional. How could such a talented player, who had really played well, become so bad so quickly?

We made an analysis of the situation. It turned out that Torbjörn had flopped a number of times on receiving the ball and immediately finding a player at his back. This situation is not that uncommon in modern football, to say the least. Torbjörn's fear of failing grew every time he failed until finally he would take no risks at all, as though paralysed by the fear of making yet another mistake. Performance anxiety had defeated ambition.

However, through the mental training I introduced, Torbjörn not only regained his ability, he also developed it. It got so that he looked forward to being attacked from behind so that he could defy and confuse his opponents. Torbjörn played a big part in IFK Gothenburg's UEFA Cup triumph some years later – the greatest achievement by a Swedish club.

It can be said that there are four personality types, with different strengths of ambition and performance anxiety. This can apply not only to individuals but to whole teams – even clubs and businesses.

The Four Personalities

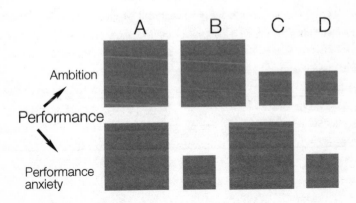

This is what it means:

A has great ambition and high performance anxiety.

B has great ambition, but is not afraid of failing.

C has little ambition and is afraid of making mistakes.

D has little ambition, but is also not bothered about failing.

Which of these four types will make the most of his resources?

D will achieve the least. It should be obvious that whoever shows neither ambition nor performance anxiety is not going to generate any kind of energy.

C will be next in achievement. C will at least use his energy not to make mistakes. It's unfortunate, but we believe that many people are like C: they devote more energy to preventing mistakes than to taking risks in order to succeed. We can leave aside C and D now as we know that the athletes we're interested in all have great ambition.

> *Accelerating and braking at the same time*

That leaves us with A and B. A steps on the accelerator and brakes at the same time. He has great ambition, which gives him drive – but at the same time his performance anxiety pulls him in the opposite direction. A is the type who is fine in ordinary league matches but fades away when it really matters.

B is, not surprisingly, the type who makes the most of his resources. B dares to excel when it really matters. So it's a question of working to be a B type and creating a B culture, and this we do by stimulating ambition and reducing fear.

> *Typical winners look like this*

Railo:

A question: how many of the players you have met on the continent are A types, and how many are B types?

Eriksson:

That's not an easy one to answer, but to give a rough idea, I would say that 80 per cent are A types, with only 20 per cent B types. So most players tend to accelerate and brake at the same time.

Railo:

What would you say is typical of players with high performance anxiety?

Eriksson:

They get desperate when they miss goals, they get mad with themselves and their team-mates and, not least, with the referee. Players like this are dangerous, as their negative fear can spread like fire to others in the team, provoking performance anxiety in everyone.

> *Fair-weather players are dangerous for a team*

Another thing that is typical of players with performance anxiety is that they depend on things going well. They are typical 'fair-weather' players in that they can do very well indeed as long as they are riding the wave of success. But when the going gets tough, everything comes to a halt and nothing will go right.

On the other hand, players with low performance anxiety can maintain their self-belief and level of performance in the midst of a setback. And that is an extremely important quality.

Now comes the question: how do you become a B type?

Security in facing challenges

Railo:

Performance anxiety is closely connected with security. People with great inner security often have little performance anxiety. And without security, we won't want to risk anything.

At the same time, we are constantly being faced with challenges, which in a way can be said to be the opposite of security. Every time we venture to reach greater heights, we risk losing our footing. And our security is threatened.

Inner security and stimulating challenges

We might consider what challenges we have set ourselves in the last few years. Are we satisfied with them? Should we have aimed higher? If we didn't try something – was it because we somehow felt that our security was threatened?

By simply looking for security we run the risk of stagnation and self-satisfaction. Actually, we need the two things – inner security and stimulating challenges. We should also realise that security is not something we will always have, regardless of the situation in which we find ourselves. We have to find different ways of reinforcing and maintaining our security.

Eriksson:

At Benfica I had a player, Alves, who always played with black gloves on. The kit manager had forgotten the gloves for one of his matches, which led Alves to declare: 'Without my black gloves I'm not going onto the field.'

I think this had something to do with an old promise to his grandfather, but it was also his way of building security, in this case by means of an external aid. I have a heap of similar stories, where pure superstition was turned into a form of security.

> ## Chance can change our minds for us

Lazio has a team manager whose name is Mauricio Mancini. Once, when we had to travel from our Formello training ground to the airport for an important away match, a road accident meant we had to make a detour as the traffic was blocked. But we made the plane in time – and won the difficult away match.

From then on, when we had to travel to important away matches, Mauricio would always arrange to take the longer route, giving traffic jams as an excuse. Finally I said something. 'How is it that there's a problem with the traffic just when we have to go to the airport?' I asked him. Then the truth emerged. Mancini was superstitious. He fully believed that we would win if we travelled by the longer route.

Railo:

Our degree of security depends on two things:

1. Our personality.
2. Our social environment.

Let's take an example: a player with high performance anxiety feels insecure and is primarily dependent on the social atmosphere around the team – but also on the security he gets from his coach and the environment. This makes him very sensitive to changes in his social environment. If everything goes as it should and his environment gives him the security he needs, the player can be successful. But if he suddenly gets less security from his environment, this player's performance anxiety will increase, and his play will suffer. This is why so many players play below their capability when they come to clubs and teams with low inner security and little emotional support.

So if as many as 80 per cent of élite players are of type A – that is, they have high performance anxiety – you can understand how important it is for them, if they are to make the most of their potential, to have security from their environment.

> Only one in five has a winning mentality

Eriksson:

This reminds me of a mistake I once made. When I went to Roma, I tried to put an end to the custom of meeting at a hotel before our Sunday matches. When we finished training one Saturday, I told the players: 'See you at lunch tomorrow.'

This caused general astonishment, and, in the end, I had to reinstate these meetings: *'Retiro!'* On the one hand, the club management was very dubious, and on the other, there was a player who felt insecure when they were not able to prepare mentally in an hotel room. Ritual and habit can provide security.

Aim to win but accept defeat

'You must dare to fail if you are to dare to succeed.'

Please read that sentence again. This may be confusing to many people. Do you really have to dare to fail to be able to succeed? And what do we mean by 'dare to succeed'?

Surely everyone dares to succeed? Unfortunately, this is not so.

As we said earlier, the promise of great success often founders on the protests of our subconscious. We feel troubled and risk landing outside something we call the 'security zone'.

Everyone has physical and mental limits. We would reach these limits if we were able to access all our resources, talents and abilities. But we also have a minimum limit. If everything went horrendously, we wouldn't be able to feel worse than our minimum limit allowed. A poor result which took us to our minimum limit would be a painful experience. We would be stricken by insecurity.

> *Our security zone must be wide*

As long as we remain above this level, we can feel secure. The interesting thing is that we erect a mental limit to protect us from our maximum. We would feel insecure if we were to exceed this. We would find ourselves completely at a loss. So it's only between our upper and lower limits that we feel completely secure.

We can see how this looks in the illustration below.

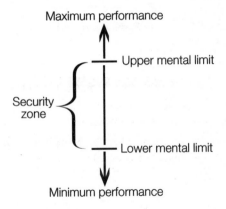

We call this the security zone. All our work in achieving better performance is really to extend this security zone – both upwards and downwards. And normally we begin with our lower mental limit.

Railo:

Athletes normally contact me wanting to improve their performance. They want to raise their upper mental limit. I usually tell them: 'We won't start there. We'll begin by dropping your lower mental limit. You'll have the security of overcoming greater failures than you have experienced so far.'

I often hear: 'Hold on. Aren't things bad enough already? Surely I shouldn't be trying to make them worse?' But that's exactly how it is. In order to raise our upper mental limit, we generally have first to drop our lower limit. This is not about changing goals. That's a completely different thing. Here we're talking about extending the security zone – both downwards and upwards.

We have good examples in ball sports of how the two boundaries work together. If we're afraid of missing, we'll also find it difficult to hit those winning shots. But if we dare to miss, we'll also dare to hit the winners. We must dare to fail in order to win.

> *Hate to lose but don't be afraid to lose*

When I lecture on this subject around the world, I often hear protests from the audience. They will say 'Surely a winner always hates to lose?' And my answer is, yes, a winner hates to lose, but a winner must not get into a state of anxiety about losing. Herein lies a very important point. If we are to be winners, we must hate to lose, but we mustn't suffer anxiety if we do.

Eriksson:

Take two players like Roberto Mancini (who is now coach of Fiorentina) and Sinisa Mihajlovic for example. They have this will to win and, obviously, they hate to lose. But they don't take defeat to heart and their anxiety is just as low when they turn up for the next match. If we look at other sports, tennis for example, we see that Björn Borg and Mats Wilander were both of this type. In golf, we can say the same thing about Tiger Woods.

> *Tiger Woods can handle winning – and losing*

These players hate to lose, but don't suffer anxiety if they do. If our performance anxiety rises, our lower mental limit is pressed upwards – at the same time as our upper limit is pressed downwards. Then we get something that we call a 'performance cage'.

An athlete often has a great deal more potential than he manages to use, but his fear of failing locks him into his performance cage. Real winners seldom suffer from this, as they succeed in keeping their performance anxiety low.

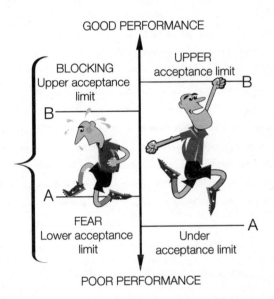

Let's look at an example outside sport. Suppose that we have put a 20-cm-wide iron girder on the floor and ask you to walk along it. No problem, right? But then we fix the same iron girder 30 metres up in the air and ask you to do the same thing. Physically, objectively, the task is no more difficult, but the fear of falling means that your performance will be much worse – you will in fact run a great risk of falling.

The more afraid you are of falling, the worse you will perform the task.

The greater our fear of making a mistake, the greater the likelihood that we will make a mistake.

Railo:

The performances of certain competition shooters offer another interesting example. When I looked at their series of shots, five shots per series, I could see that they often missed towards the end. If they had three or four tens, the fifth tended to be a seven or eight. Their subconscious would begin to protest, saying 'Hey, you're not that good!' After a few bulls'-eyes they would get this feeling that they were on the way to landing outside their upper mental limit and they would start to feel insecure. So they would miss. And that miss would feel great. Back to security again, down to the security zone.

We carried out an experiment. When the shooters had shot three bulls'-eyes, we broke off the series and told them we'd take a break, that we'd start again afterwards. The shooters again shot three tens – no problem. But of course they had now shot six tens in a row. The reason, as everyone will realise, was purely psychological and not technical. The subconscious accepts shooting three tens in a row, but not five, and certainly not eight tens in a row. The subconscious puts on the brakes. And this subconscious brake governs our will, which would love to have as many tens as possible.

> *The subconscious puts on the brakes*

Anyone who has played golf or tennis will know of many situations where subconscious mental processes dominate the will and conscious processes.

So what should we do? Well, there are only three possible paths. Let's take a high jumper as an example.

1. He can elect not to jump at all. That's going to be the surest way of not hitting the bar – of not making a mistake. Unfortunately, we see people taking this way out all too often: never jump, never venture, never dare or have a go, never accept a challenge.

2. He can set the bar so low that he's bound to make the height. A safe way out, but not particularly constructive.

3. He can set the bar high. Now there is a great risk of hitting the bar.

And he certainly will hit it a few times. But to develop he must – as we must – test himself at the margins of his expertise.

Ronaldo – impossible to win duels against him

Eriksson:

What kind of psychological mechanisms prevent people from achieving their goals, or a team from winning an important match, just as they are about to 'cross the line'?

Railo:

Mental blocks are a problem which I have worked with for many years, inside and outside the world of sport. A mental block is often established when a person experiences something very negative in connection with a particular situation.

When I was working with a Manchester United player, I asked him to close his eyes and imagine that he was playing against Ronaldo. I also asked him to create a number of mental images in which he won duels against Ronaldo.

After ten minutes I asked the player to tell me how he felt. There were two things that he told me:

1. It was impossible to win duels against Ronaldo.

2. He suffered anxiety when he had mentally to work with the situation.

To me, this was a clear example of a mental block. If he couldn't, even in his mind, 'see' how to beat Ronaldo, how would he ever do it in reality?

> ## The brain registers and stores

The brain is like a large storeroom, with an almost endless number of impulses, impressions, experiences, pieces of knowledge, thoughts and feelings that have been registered from birth. The greater part of our basic character is determined during childhood, as well as the way we are perceived by our parents. Our role in life has already been defined. It is then that we learn how to perceive our own person.

This is then reinforced or weakened through the years. Whatever we learned from our parents, teachers, comrades and trainers remains in our mental storeroom and will almost certainly affect our performances. To a certain extent, we can consciously retrieve and use things. But most things affect us subconsciously. Our brain registers and stores. Then it exerts its influence subconsciously.

Our brain systematically connects things that take place at the same time.

A footballer who misses important penalties soon begins to connect penalties with misses. And the next time he has to take a penalty in an important match, his psyche will 'tell' him that he is going to miss.

He suffers from a block that first of all forces him to miss again.

If a player always does well at one stadium but believes that he won't at another, the pattern will often continue as he expects it to.

The skier who imagines that his technique is better suited to certain slalom slopes but not to others will tend to have results that bear this out.

The good news is that all of this can actually be changed, since the opposite is also true: the player who always puts penalties away has a brain which 'tells' him that he won't be missing next time, either. Negative impulses can be trained to be positive. The energy that has ground us down can also lift us up.

> ## Our brain has a phenomenal ability to change

A culture of winning: Sven-Göran Eriksson celebrates Lazio's win in Italy's Serie A in May 2000. Lazio had not won lo Scudetto for 26 years.

Give us a smile: Interest in Sven's appointment as manager of the England national team was enormous following his presentation to the media in November 2000.

Right-hand man: Fellow Swede Tord Grip has worked with Sven-Göran Eriksson for many years at various clubs throughout Europe.

A helping hand: Steve McClaren and Peter Taylor, who looked after the England team temporarily, continued to help with the team even when Sven arrived in February 2001.

Olà Sven: Once again the media watch closely as Sven-Göran Eriksson oversees the preparations for his first match as England manager, a friendly against Spain at Villa Park.

Flying start: Nicky Barmby scores England's first goal against Spain. Emile Heskey and Ugo Ehiogu scored the other goals to give England a 3–0 win.

My left foot: Pundits said Sven-Göran Eriksson needed to resolve England's lack of a good left-back. He solved this by bringing in Ashley Cole (above left) and Chris Powell (right).

Leading by example: David Beckham is congratulated by his team-mates after scoring against Finland in Sven-Göran Eriksson's first World Cup qualifying match at Anfield.

One down: Michael Owen slots the first goal for England past Albania's goalkeeper in Tirana in their 3–1 win.

Two to go: Paul Scholes gets England's second goal against Albania.

Three to finish: Andrew Cole silences his critics with his first goal for England and the team's third goal in their win against Albania.

Training in Spain: Sven-Göran Eriksson and Tord Grip observe the England team as they go through their exercise regime during a brief get-together in the sun before setting off for their next match against Greece.

Greek tragedy: At least that's what it was for the hosts, as England took their winning tally of World Cup qualifying match wins to three out of three, helped by a deft goal from Paul Scholes.

Tense times: The England coaching staff watch from the 'bench' during the match against Greece in Athens. England eventually won 2–0.

Brilliant Becks: The England captain adds the final touch by scoring the second goal against Greece.

Our brain has a phenomenal ability to change its stock, to switch from minus to plus and to direct with positive impulses instead of negative ones.

In football, we can discern three different kinds of block:

1. Goal blocks.

2. Situation blocks.

3. Technique blocks.

We previously mentioned Torbjörn Nilsson, the Swedish player who played very poorly during his professional stint in Holland. The reason, as we said, was that he failed on several occasions when he got a player at his back, and then suffered a block every time this situation repeated itself.

Others can be affected by a mental block when they play away on a particular pitch. The brain may have connected an unpleasant experience with this pitch through fear.

This kind of situational block can easily take hold because every time it happens, the player or the team will receive an unconscious reinforcement of the block. It is not as though this phenomenon is inconsistent, as it tends to repeat itself. This in turn can lead to a mental deadlock.

What we have just described are blocks that result from emotional reactions, fear and anxiety. But we can also have intellectual blocks. If our brain continually thinks a negative thought connected to a certain situation, the same thing will happen: our subconscious will block.

I once worked with a forward in the Italian League who only scored about four goals every season.

His problem was that he had scored on average around 18 goals per season in the team he was bought from. I analysed the situation and found that he had established both intellectual and emotional blocks, but that these were first triggered when he came to a team who played at a higher level than the one he was accustomed to. He began to think:

'It will be hard for me to assert myself in this team. It will be hard for me to score goals in the league. I feel that I'm not as good as many players in my own team, never mind about Milan or Juventus.'

His mental blocks decreed that he should score no more than four goals per season. This was what his subconscious block had dictated. And when the psychological aspect says 'stop', so do the physical and technical aspects.

I have worked with players who, when they approach the goal, think the goalkeeper grows into a giant and that the goal becomes smaller and smaller. Another player would mentally visualise how he was shooting at goal – but the ball went wide every time. When he tried to picture the ball going in, this felt remarkable, odd, and he was ridden with anxiety.

This is an example of a technical block. In the chapter on mental training later in the book, we describe the method I used to solve this problem. I also have many examples of situational blocks, such as when a player has only the goalkeeper to beat, or mental blocks, when a particular opponent or goalkeeper is the problem. Many players also have a 'home ground – away ground' block. There are a huge number of examples from various sports.

Eriksson:

Let me go back in time to the three seasons when I trained Degerfors in Sweden, the first of these seasons with Tord Grip, who used to help me at Lazio before becoming my assistant with England. It was then that I called on Willi Railo for the first time, and our collaboration began.

We won the series two years in a row, but then lost in the qualifier. Our team always played fantastically well in the series, but as soon as it came to the qualifier, we'd mess up. One Saturday, Willi came and worked with us for the whole day. He made a cassette for individual players, so that they could practise mental training on their own. We even used to stop the bus on the way to away matches so that players could use their cassettes to prepare mentally. We won the series easily again – but before the qualifier the players listened carefully to their cassettes. We won the qualifier and went up a division.

Railo:

A block or mental barrier can manifest itself in a number of ways. It can lie in the borderland between thoughts and feelings. Perhaps the easiest way of dealing with a block is to learn to recognise it. It can often be found in thoughts such as:

'I never do well in the inside lane. You saw what happened last year!'

'This ground is always lousy.'

'We never do well against this team.'

'With this draw I might as well give him a bye.'

'You can't play on these dry grounds.'

Eriksson:

When I played right-back for a Swedish football team, we had a coach who discovered that we played better away than at home. His analysis of the situation was that we always went by bus to away matches.

Consequently, we were told we had to meet an hour before our home matches too – to go somewhere by bus. The bus would drive around aimlessly so that we could mentally prepare in the same way as we did for away matches.

He tried to utilise the mental block we had – that we were better away than at home. But this isn't the way to solve this kind of problem. Now I see that it is through mental training and changing the collective mentality that such problems can be solved.

Railo:

In golf and tennis, fear of hitting the ball is a well-known phenomenon.

When a match or competition is at a critical stage, many players are afraid to 'hit through' their stroke for fear of missing. They may get 'rubber arm', which makes the arm go weak and plays havoc with their technique, or they may get 'cramp arm', where they won't attempt to complete their stroke smoothly. It ends in cramp, with the obvious outcome.

> The person with the widest security zone is best

I would like to emphasise what we have stated before… we must dare to fail if we are to dare to succeed. The person with the widest security zone under pressure is also going to be the best when it matters. The problem nowadays is not a lack of ambition but rather that many people carry with them high performance anxiety. It's useless to put your foot down for all you're worth if, at the same time, you're braking with the other foot as hard as you can.

What self-image do you have?

There is a special kind of block – but also an opportunity – in the roles we play in football, various other games and, for that matter, life itself.

In every sort of social situation, we take part in a kind of theatre, with its own unwritten rules. Often, we don't even realise this, simply accepting that it is so.

We don't choose the role we play by ourselves. Of course we try, consciously and unconsciously, to create the role that we would like to play, but others also give us our role. There is a very strong social force in others' expectations and evaluations of us – something that is evident as soon as we try to change our role.

> ## Our role affects our situation

It is often very difficult for others to accept such a change. It is also psychologically difficult for us to change our roles. At the same time, the role we play is extremely important in relation to how we succeed.

Railo:

I believe the following rule applies: 'It is difficult to perform better than our role dictates.' I don't say that it's impossible – just difficult.

Here's an example from a completely different area – the classroom. A schoolgirl was, for no apparent reason, quite mediocre at maths. So her teacher gave the whole class a test which, unbeknown to the class, he threw straight into the wastepaper basket. Then he came back to the class and told everyone that the mediocre kid had scored the highest mark. Almost immediately, this kid's role in the class began to change, and she was treated with greater respect until she herself believed that she ought to play a different role in her maths class. As a result, her marks in tests improved.

When I worked with Ingrid Kristiansen, the long-distance runner who set three world records in 1986 (5,000 metres, 10,000 metres and the marathon), her main competitor also came from Norway – Grete Waitz. She was the world number one and won the New York marathon nine times. Ingrid's problem was that she had defined her role in relation to Grete Waitz. Ingrid considered herself to be number two, with Grete number one.

Making use of mental training, I asked Ingrid to create a mental picture in which she was in the leading position in a marathon, in front of Grete.

After several minutes, Ingrid said that she simply wasn't able to create this mental picture. In her picture, Grete was number one and she was number two. When, on the other hand, I asked her to create a mental picture of herself lying second, with Grete first, it was easy to do. 'This mental picture feels natural and right,' said Ingrid.

Eriksson:

It was just like that at Lazio. It was the club itself that had defined its role, which was in a class below that of the great Italian teams: Milan, Juventus and the rest. It was therefore important for us mentally to change our role, otherwise it was going to be difficult to achieve the really big successes.

Railo:

A role like Lazio's in your example can often be developed with relatively little effort, although it takes time of course. What happens is that a player, team or club will acquire small signs which will 'tell' them what role they are to play. If we already have a role to play, we will accept the signals which conform to that role more easily than those that do not. So it is possible to step into both 'winner roles' and 'loser roles'. The coach's approach will be important here, and can function almost like a programming of the players. If the coach treats a player or team as a loser, they will often fulfil that role – and the converse is also true. A far-sighted coach will help the sportsmen to develop a positive role, making them aware of how they can develop their own winner role, as well as how to avoid the danger of taking up a loser role, whether in the good or the bad times. This happens through close collaboration between coach, player and club. A coach must create trust in the whole environment, together with a readiness to change.

Conclusion: If we are seen to be winners by others, we are more likely to be successful. If we realise this, we will also have another weapon. If we understand that we can be so easily influenced by the opinions of others, then taking steps to change ourselves, and later our role, will not appear so daunting.

Winner roles and loser roles

Fixed roles and mental blocks of all kinds clearly prevent us from fulfilling our potential. What is so interesting and encouraging, however, is that everything can be turned into a positive force.

Break through the barriers

We often find it difficult, both intellectually and emotionally, to accept a sufficiently high level for our performance. We dare not pass our upper limit and reach our maximum. We have an inner mental barrier that stops us from succeeding. We have to break through the barriers which we mentally erect, that prevent us from using all our resources.

A very good example is provided by sport's 'dream' barriers. When a sportsman breaks through one of these barriers, others follow.

For a long time, it was considered impossible to run a mile under four minutes. But Roger Bannister, from England, did so. It was not long before a number of other runners managed to run a mile in under four minutes, although there was nothing remarkable about their training. Bannister showed that it was permitted to run that quickly – and to break barriers.

It's often a courageous person, someone with vision, who self-confidently dares to follow his desire, who breaks through barriers. Such athletes are said to have great 'mental height'. That is, an unconscious acceptance of breaking barriers and maintaining a high level of performance for a long time. In the chapter on mental training, we show how everyone can work with mental training in a practical way. Any breaking through barriers first has to be done in the mind. The mind must prepare the way for the body.

A great determination to achieve one's goal is also necessary.

A person with inner conviction can attain greater mental height than other people. We took Alberto Tomba as a good example of a sportsman who competed with a greater mental height than others. Winning was for him a natural condition. For sportsmen with great mental height, winning is nothing out of the ordinary. By the same token, losing fundamentally changes nothing, and is taken with great patience: in the next competition, it feels just as natural to win again.

> Dream barriers are dangerous

Railo:

Mental height reveals the degree of inner acceptance that we have for a goal or performance – or for breaking a barrier. If the mental height does not correspond, it won't make any difference what goals we set up. Our acceptance of a goal must be intellectual, emotional and unconscious. This can be trained mentally.

> Mental height – more important than goals

Remember:

- Mental processes (thoughts, feelings, mental energy) decide who the winners and losers will be.
- Being a winner can be learnt systematically.
- Subconscious barriers prevent many people from reaching their potential.
- Ambition cannot be learnt but the will to win can be.
- The fear of making mistakes is the greatest barrier to success.
- Winners have great ambition and low performance anxiety.
- Only about 20 per cent are natural 'B-types'.
- Feelings of personal security and security in our environment are crucial.
- We must dare to fail in order to succeed.
- The amplitude of our security zone is decisive.
- Winners hate to lose, but are not afraid to lose.
- Most people have mental blocks and barriers.
- Blocks in sport concern goals, situations and technique.
- It is difficult to perform better than the role we have chosen – or been assigned – allows us to.
- Dream barriers in sport are mental blocks.

SELF-CONFIDENCE

– The most important thing of all

The Olympic Games ice hockey tournament at Lake Placid, 1980:
The 'machine' from the then Soviet Union was thought to be unbeatable. The other nations were mostly competing for silver and bronze. Nobody had even been talking about the gang of amateurs from the USA.

But it was the young, untested American team who won Olympic gold.

The 1992 European Football Championship in Sweden:
Denmark slid into the tournament on a banana skin after a Yugoslavia torn apart by civil war was forced to back out at the last moment. Denmark scraped together a team by hastily recalling a number of professionals from holiday. They were given little chance of progressing from the early rounds. Yet it was Denmark who won the European Championship title.

Eriksson:
I have seen numerous matches where the weaker team on paper beat the other team because of greater self-belief and team spirit. And the same thing is true for individual players: self-confidence and inner strength can be decisive in duels on the field, even when, objectively speaking, an opponent is the more skilful footballer.

When IFK Gothenburg were due to play Hamburg in the 1982 UEFA Cup final, I warned my players about Horst Hrubesch, their incredibly difficult and able forward. 'Watch out for him,' I said. 'He's frighteningly good with his head.' Glenn Hysén, the centre-back, came back straightaway with 'We'll buy you dinner for every time he wins a header'. That's real self-confidence for you.

Railo:
I imagine the importance of self-confidence becomes apparent when someone suddenly loses it…

Eriksson:
Then it's even more obvious. All it takes is a little bad luck in a couple of matches for a team to begin to lose faith in their own ability. It can even turn during a few

seconds of a match: a muffed penalty, some near misses, unluckily conceding a goal. The players will lose their self-confidence, and the match is lost.

I can give you another example. We managed to change the attitude at Benfica in six months. This was a team who played well at home, with a lot of courage, but as soon as they had an away game, it was a different story.

It seemed that in the Portuguese League, the team had learnt that by drawing away and winning at home, they could win the league.

The away matches in Europe were lacklustre. The players didn't want to run and challenge the opposition, and kept falling back. Finally, during a UEFA Cup match against Betis Sevilla, I lost my temper. We were losing 0–1, but the players were as pleased as punch. Losing 0–1 was OK, 0–0 was even better – because we would beat them at home.

At half-time I was furious, and gave them all a telling-off. 'What are you trying to do?' I said. 'Are you here to play football or not?' 'Sure,' said one of the players, 'but this is how we play away from home.'

So I said: 'The field is no bigger here than it is at home, the grass is the same. If you can play football at home, you must be able to play football here.'

We turned the match round, won 2–1 and reached the final of the UEFA Cup. We lost in the final but at least we were able to change our attitude to away matches. I talked to the players a lot, and they played with spirit in the away matches too. The team's self-confidence rose dramatically. We won the league both years and the cup once.

How do we build self-confidence?

Railo:

Self-confidence depends both on our own personality and the situation in which we find ourselves. Personal self-confidence depends on whether:

• We feel accepted as a person, both in prosperity and adversity.

- We have had basic human love from our parents.
- We have had the confidence to take on responsibility.
- We have felt free within strict limits.
- We have felt that someone believed in our talent and prospects.

> *Personal self-confidence remains stable*

This kind of self-confidence remains relatively stable through the years.

But in addition to this, there is the self-confidence that is connected to situations and other people. This may swing suddenly, depending on our experience and training.

There are lots of examples of how this special kind of self-confidence is developed. A footballer can be self-confident with his right foot, but not so with his left. Some people exhibit self-confidence at home but none at all playing away. We can be full of self-confidence when we head the ball, but have none at all when we dribble. There can be self-confidence in attack, but not in defence. We can be full of self-confidence against certain players, but have none at all against others. All of this is due to the fact that we collect experience that is stored in the brain. It is therefore important to store the right things.

Unfortunately, we see many coaches and players destroying self-confidence by always looking for faults and being too negative. Too much energy is spent correcting faults instead of reinforcing what is good.

Coaches become 'no-fixated' instead of 'yes-encouraging'.

For example, a team who were favourites in the league lost a number of matches and it was apparent to many people that although they played well in certain respects, they committed too many simple errors. Their coach, however, chose to train still harder on the things the team already did well and completely ignored their mistakes. In this way, the team's self-confidence was reinforced – and they started to win again.

Building self- confidence

It is much easier to build up a particular self-confidence than to retrieve a generally lagging self-confidence. Obviously, it is also easier to build up a particular self-confidence if there is already self-belief from the beginning.

The success of all this depends however not only on strictly sporting success – it is also bound up with how our coach, team-mates and others, react to our success or misfortune.

Railo:

I once worked with a wrestler who qualified for the world championships. At home in Scandinavia, he performed with great self-confidence and generally won. When he went to the world championships, it didn't go badly – it went really badly.

He said, 'When I compete in Scandinavia, I feel strong and my self-confidence is good both before a competition and during the bouts.

'But when I came here to the world championships, I saw a Russian and it was like my arms withered away. I had no strength, lost all my energy and felt feeble when I got onto the mat. My self-confidence had completely vanished.'

Self-confidence which depends on our social environment shows how difficult it can be sometimes to maintain a belief in ourselves. There are footballers with good general self-confidence – and good specific self-confidence in several areas – who lose their belief in their ability when they are in a negative environment.

A player's self-confidence may be good when he's playing for his club but poor when he's playing for his country. Many players lose their self-confidence when a new coach joins their club. New routines are introduced, there's a different kind of team spirit, a different environment.

A very talented player moved from a small Scandinavian club to one of the great continental clubs. His success had been immediate, built as it was on a very fast, aggressive and technically assured game. But the change was tough. This player had come from a very secure environment, where he knew everybody, talked to everybody, and was given great encouragement. In his new club, everything was different: the culture, the language, the team, the coach and, not least, the pressure. His game began to suffer, he was hesitant and lacking in initiative – all because his self-confidence had sunk like a stone. And the worse he played, the more often he sat out on the bench.

Eriksson:

What can we do to ensure that the self-confidence a player has built up is not destroyed?

Railo:

The coach plays a very important role here. His system of reward and punishment, his ability to create team spirit and support the group, will largely determine whether a player retains his self-confidence in match situations. The kind of self-confidence which is most resistant combines the three aspects we have talked about: good, basic and general security, different specific and acquired kinds of self-confidence, and a supportive social environment.

Keeping self-confidence high in adversity

Unfortunately, there are many examples of coaches who, particularly in adversity, destroy their players' self-confidence. This is easy to do. If we withdraw support for a player, deliver negative criticism and begin to send out signals that we doubt his ability, there are soon going to be enormous negative consequences for his self-confidence. And if a player is exposed to this treatment, he'll find it easy to go along with the pattern and will start to punish himself. We can be unduly self-critical, and in the end we can be our worst enemy.

> ### Accept your players in adversity as well

Sometimes you hear a sportsman say 'I'm my worst critic'. We should of course be self-critical, but not in a destructive way. The positive idea we have of ourselves can suffer, often resulting in a guilty conscience.

A guilty conscience characterises many people who have lived under compulsion and with thoughts such as 'I must, I should, I shall', rather than the liberating 'I want to, I'll have a go, I can'. We must look for a realistic and constructive reaction to defeat. No one wants you to be happy after a loss. And it's not an easy time to come up with positive thoughts and feelings. But, as everyone who devotes himself to sport will sooner or later suffer adversity, it's important to handle the situation properly.

Instead of allowing it to be destructive, a setback can be used for constructive training and for building up concentration and motivation.

Think about self-confidence as being important for concentration. Imagine a damaging inner spiral which begins with poor self-confidence, continues with a negative way of thinking, and then produces high mental tension, which leads to a lack of concentration. In this context, it is our self-confidence, rather than our concentration, which must be worked on. We must tackle the cause, not the symptom. Remember too, that there is a definite difference between 'hating to lose' and 'daring to lose'. The best sportsmen have both reactions within themselves. That is, they use their 'hate' to build up motivation for the next competition.

> ### Tackle the cause not the symptom

Self-confidence, not conceit

Eriksson:

I'll go along with that. But sometimes it seems like certain players or teams have too much self-confidence, and this has negative consequences. What do you think?

Railo:

I don't think you can have too much self-confidence. On the other hand, self-confidence can easily become something else. I mean conceit, being cocky, self-centred and arrogant – words that are, unfortunately, often confused with self-confidence. We know that the successful person, in whatever walk of life, is always in danger of losing his humility. It is simply humility that separates self-confidence, which is positive, from conceit, which is dangerous.

Eriksson:

What is it exactly that happens when we become conceited and arrogant – and, in consequence, lose?

Railo:

We become so certain that success is going to follow, that we end up having low mental energy. We stop concentrating, so the quality of what we are doing – training as well as competing – goes down. We feel that we no longer have to try, that success will come anyway. Conceit also leads to a defensive attitude: while before we attacked to win, we now try to defend our previous successes.

> *Conceit and arrogance are not the same as self-confidence*

All of this means that it is incredibly important for a coach to bring his players back to earth, to begin from zero in every match and every season.

There is nothing wrong with a healthy self-confidence, as long as we retain our humility and an attacking mentality.

This is a good moment for an old Chinese proverb: 'Whoever is not crazed by success neither will be broken by adversity.'

Self-confidence should not be confused with other, rather similar concepts.

Let us look at the differences:

SELF-CONFIDENCE consists of three parts:
- We accept ourselves – the good as well as the bad.
- We firmly believe in our resources.
- We have a fundamental security.

COCKINESS is often a defence mechanism for people with poor self-confidence. For instance, to be able to reveal that we are insecure often requires a good deal of self-confidence.

SELF-CENTREDNESS means that we believe that the world revolves around us. Also a sign of poor self-confidence.

CONCEIT is shown by people who not only accept themselves uncritically, but also overestimate their own worth. They only see their good side, and never the bad.

ARROGANCE is used by people who have to push others down in order to raise themselves up.

There are countless examples in sport of how arrogance and conceit reduce the ability to perform. As another proverb says: 'Pride goes before a fall.'

Railo:

I know that you have a pennant at home dating from 1982. Tell us about that.

Eriksson:

It was when I was the coach of IFK Gothenburg and we were preparing for the final of the UEFA Cup against Hamburg. The Germans were so convinced that they were going to win that they sold pennants before the match with the words: 'Hamburg – UEFA Cup winners 1982'. But we won the match and were the champions. I wonder what Hamburg did with all those pennants?

> *Arrogance is used to push others down*

The big question is: how do you create self-confidence? Let's turn the concept of self-confidence round and look at it from another angle. We could say that self-confidence is actually being able to have control over oneself and one's performance. This viewpoint has several consequences, both for how we create self-confidence and how we can keep it under pressure.

It is usual, and understandable, for us to connect our own person with our performance. But I believe in just the opposite: separate the person from the performance. Our performance is always going to vary – nobody can always be at the top.

The problem with connecting the performance to the person is that our view of ourselves will go up and down with our performance, so that we become the victims of our own performances. With mental training, we can have control over ourselves and our performance, instead of becoming a victim of our performance.

> *Separate the person from the performance*

Thermometers

Self-confidence is often the basis for everything else. It often becomes easier to concentrate and to motivate ourselves, our form is affected positively, we become less nervous and our temperament improves. Let us look at some 'thermometers' which reveal the state of our self-confidence.

Motivation

Self-confidence is intimately connected with motivation.

When our motivation goes down, it can be a sign that our self-confidence is beginning to sink. If we no longer really believe in ourselves, neither will we believe in what we do – and our motivation will unconsciously go down.

Eriksson:

When I was coach with Fiorentina we met Napoli away one Wednesday in the cup – and won the game. Diego Maradona had mostly loafed about for 90 minutes on the field, but after the match he came up to me and said, 'Congratulations on the win, mister, but on Sunday you'll be dancing to a different tune.' We met Napoli again four days later – this time in the league. We weren't given a chance. Napoli won 5–0 and Maradona was brilliant throughout the match.

Our left-back came to the bench and asked me in desperation, 'What should I do about Maradona?'

'Beats me,' I replied.

That just shows what motivation can do. Maradona was simply incredibly motivated in the league match, but not in the cup match.

Another example took place with Lazio in the 1997–98 season. We got to the final of the Italian Cup, were on the way to the final of the UEFA Cup and were well placed in the league. Then the team lost at home in the league match against Juventus. When our players realised that they could no longer win the league, their motivation just evaporated. Our seven last league matches said it all: six defeats and one draw.

Railo:

Were you able to mobilise new energy for your cup matches?

Eriksson:

Yes, against Milan at home in the cup final. We won it, which was a great success for Lazio, who hadn't won anything big for several years. The champagne was flowing and though we still had important games to come, there was a feeling that the season was over after that match. In the final of the UEFA Cup, against Inter in Paris, the team couldn't get going. We were mentally dead and Inter won easily 3–1.

Railo:

Motivation has to be built with a number of building blocks:

- Trust is the foundation. Everyone in the club has to be open, honest and strive for fairness. Respect must be shown to everyone as an independent individual.
- The 'we' feeling. This is particularly the leader's responsibility. If the leader sets up conditions ('If you're going to be in *my* team, then you'd better...'), the active member is excluded and is left unmotivated.
- Variation in training. New methods, new places, other sports. Monotony is out.
- Participation in the planning of match and training programmes. Active members must be able to take part in discussions.
- Everyone's views must be valued. Active members must not have the feeling that everything is decided in advance during closed board meetings or secret discussions in corridors.
- Openness and clear information. We must be able to talk openly about anything – including problems.
- Encouragement. Supporting and helping team-mates should be an obvious part of instruction and training.
- More play. As a further variation to training, the trainer can opt for play situations. Change livens people up – and increases motivation. When there is a lack of motivation, for example in a team, the social environment has to be analysed extremely carefully. Small conflicts can often lead to great wars.

For example, a football team had a great team spirit and plenty of motivation. Results went accordingly – very good. But at the same time, the coach discovered that two or three players were beginning to lose their motivation. He couldn't understand why. During their training sessions he had treated everybody equally, believing this was only fair. But now it turned out that the players had private problems. One of them had problems at work. Another had a problem with his girlfriend. The danger in such situations is that poor spirits, or discontent, spreads from two or three players to the rest of the team. The solution is to give individuals more attention. 'Monotonous' and 'relentless' are not words associated with good leadership.

> *Give individual attention*
> *Concentration*

If you manage to concentrate 100 per cent of the time, you can stop reading now!

Your mind will be in excellent condition and you won't need to improve your mental competitiveness. In our opinion, however, very few people achieve total concentration. In simple terms, concentration involves the direction of our thoughts towards a definite, delimited area, while at the same time succeeding in excluding other areas. Concentration therefore lends itself particularly well to mental training.

> *Concentration must be trained*

We train the part of our body that we need to – a jumper trains his legs, a javelin thrower his arm. We are not as dedicated to mental training.

Our concentration can be disturbed by so many things, on and off the field. Someone in the crowd screams something that stays in our mind and our thoughts turn around that, and not on the game. Many sportsmen having to compete in new environments have started to use 'model training': training somewhere which replicates the new environment as closely as possible.

Railo:

I have worked with Eirik Kvalfoss, the biathlon athlete, who had problems with his concentration in certain situations, such as when spectators booed when he missed. The home crowd was particularly difficult. I taped the sound of the fans during competitions and had him listen to it, using earphones, during his normal physical training, but also while relaxing at home as part of his mental training. The result was that he was able to deal with the public during his next competition – and maintain his concentration. He took gold, silver and bronze at the Sarajevo Olympics.

Another thing that disturbs our concentration is if we think too much about the score in a competition or match, instead of directing all our oncentration to whatever requires our attention at that moment. The Swedish tennis player Björn Borg had a phenomenal ability to forget the point he last played, regardless of whether he had won or lost it, and to concentrate on the ball that was in the air.

Basically, good or bad form is simply a sign of something else – self-confidence, motivation, mood, mental energy.

Mood

Our mood is perhaps the best barometer of how our self-confidence is going. When players begin to argue with their team-mates or the referee, we can be sure that their ability to perform is on the decline. But it need not come to such strong reactions. Solemnity also disturbs concentration and impairs performance. Many people seem to think that to be serious about sport is to have the demeanour of an undertaker. Joking is practically forbidden by some coaches. But experience shows that the best results are built on a foundation of enjoyment.

Enjoyment – not solemnity

Railo:

The coach's job is important here. It's all about preserving that element of fun. Training sessions shouldn't be monotonously boring. I know of a case where a Swedish goalkeeper was playing really well for his club, then had to represent the national team in an important tournament. Things didn't go well at all. He let in a lot of goals and came in for a lot of criticism. When he returned to his club for the next match his coach told him: 'I want you to go in and enjoy it today. I don't care if you let in ten goals – as long as you try to enjoy yourself!' The goalkeeper absolutely nailed up his goal and had one of his best matches ever.

The French player Nicolas Anelka was sold by Arsenal to Real Madrid, a deal involving well over £20 million. Anelka had been enormously successful with Arsenal but in Spain he found the going tough, and began to play below his ability. In an interview, he said:

'I'm only 20 and should be having fun out on the field. But it's not like that now. And when I'm not enjoying it, I find it hard to play at my best.'

Remember:

- Self-confidence is the most important psychological factor in your performance.
- Self-confidence is dependent on your basic personality, various situations, and other people.
- Self-confidence is governed by security, which is dependent on your social environment – especially in adversity.
- Adversity can be utilised for positive training.
- Self-confidence is positive, while conceit is negative.
- Enjoyment is a factor in performance.
- Seriousness is a different thing to solemnity.
- Self-confidence can be actively worked on.
- 'Whoever is not crazed by success will neither be broken by adversity.'

MENTAL ENERGY

– Coping with pressure

Eriksson:

I once had a player in one of my teams who was selected for the national team. Just as in my team, he was also very good in training with the national side. He showed excellent skills, took the initiative in the penalty area and had that rare ability to be in the right place when there was a chance of a goal. But then it was time for the international match. I could swear it wasn't the same person. He was passive and seemed to lack concentration, made many bad passes and didn't move like he usually did. After only 25 minutes he was substituted. When he came back to me, I discussed the matter with him and had my suspicions confirmed. He was too tense and charged up.

Mental tension and energy

Railo:

Excessive mental tension is one of the biggest problems that sportsmen have on important occasions, often producing a mental block. There is a risk that what we have learnt during training – technique and tactics – will disappear. Therefore it is important to make sure that technique and tactics are second nature to us, so that everything will go smoothly even when our mental tension is high.

> High mental tension causes mental blocks

Excessive mental tension will affect our touch and our ability to perceive and to evaluate, so naturally it will be difficult to make the right decisions on the football pitch.

To many sportsmen it is like having an alien spirit in the body. Excessive tension not only results in physical, technical and mental blocks, it also reduces our self-confidence. The question, then, is how to deal with pressure.

One thing is clear: it is difficult to change our environment. Journalists will continue to write, the public to demand victories, club directors to want to see results. So we aren't able to do very much about external pressures.

The golden rule is therefore: the greater the outer pressure, the more important it is to reduce the inner pressure.

We can reduce inner pressure by:

- Limiting expectations and demands.
- Working hard with the 'we' feeling and inner solidarity.
- Stopping internal criticism.
- Stimulating constructive thinking.
- Working with our mental attitudes.

It is also important to remember that the converse holds. The lower the outer pressure, the more important it is to increase the inner pressure. This can best be done by:

- Making greater demands.
- Raising our goals.
- Running through the consequences of lack of sharpness.
- Overestimating our opponent's prospects of winning.
- Putting the most out-of-touch players on the bench.
- Changing the team.
- Stimulating attacking thinking.

Eriksson:

I have observed the consequences of low mental tension on many occasions. When I coached IFK Gothenburg we succeeded in winning the UEFA Cup in May 1982, one of the biggest successes a Swedish club team has ever had, internationally. We had the right tension then. The week after, we met an average Swedish side – and lost. Why? Well, our mental tension was too low.

Before the World Cup finals in France, the Brazilian team went to Norway for an international. Norway won by as much as 4–2 against the future World Cup finalists.

Obviously, the Brazilian players' mental tension was too low and produced too little mental energy. Norway, on the other hand, took the match seriously and succeeded in generating mental tension.

Railo:

Some sportsmen feel good under pressure. Others go under because of it.

The point is to find the correct balance in our mental tension. Both excessive and insufficient levels of tension will lead to inferior levels of performance. More work has to be done individually here. Some people can take a lot of pressure and actually improve. You only have to think about the best Formula One drivers, who become cooler and cooler the faster they go. Other people can only take a little pressure and become more stressed as the pressure rises. Such people need more security and support from their social environment.

> *Low mental tension – low motivation*

There are examples of sportsmen who have no trouble at all with pressure.

They raise their performance in important competitions and have the ability to be best when it counts. But unfortunately, there are many more examples of sportsmen that are the exact opposite. They set world records in local competitions but don't stand a chance at the Olympics or a world championship. They'll score ten penalties in a row in training, but they'll miss in an important cup match. They look feeble instead of being charged up and raring to go. They lack the ability to mobilise their mental energy at the right moment.

The more I worked with this graph, the more important I realised that it was for coaches and players to work to regulate their mental tension.

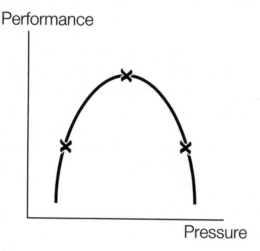

Performance

Pressure

Eriksson:

What actually affects mental tension. Is it simply external and internal pressures?

Railo:

There are also a number of other factors. But their effect can vary:

ENJOYMENT – affects tension positively, so should always be sought out.

MOTIVATION – also has a positive effect. But we can sometimes become over-motivated, with negative consequences.

AGGRESSION – definitely increases mental tension, but is negative. Aggression blocks a number of areas: technique, tactics, concentration, assessment.

Have you found this?

Eriksson:

Absolutely. That's why it's so important to motivate each other and keep the fun of playing foremost in our minds, regardless of results. I spend a lot of energy taking the aggression out of my players. All a player has to do is begin to argue with the referee, play dirty or quarrel with the opposition for there to be a danger that their performance level will sink like a stone – not only the player's performance, the whole team's.

> *Keep the fun of playing in mind*

Lazio got hammered

Railo:

Mental tension will also greatly affect mental energy. Mental energy is really important where our ability to perform is concerned. You could compare mental energy with a Ferrari engine. However good it might be, without the right petrol, ignition and timing it's not going to reach its full potential.

One way to create mental energy is through mental tension and positive pressure. A runner I worked with promised the media before the world championships that she would set a new world record. This of course created huge outside pressure: from the media, the public, sponsors, coach and competitors.

But this runner simply wanted to take the initiative in creating a lot of mental energy. And she did set that new world record.

Eriksson:

I can give you a very good example of Lazio's failure to build up mental energy for a match. We really got hammered against Valencia in the Champions' League, in April 2000: 2–5 away. We conceded two goals during the first three minutes – before I had even had time to sit down on the bench. Why did it happen? Because of our game programme before the match – and my mistakes.

Before the Valencia match we had first met Chelsea away in the Champions'

League, and won 2–1. Then we played an important derby against Roma at home. We had lost badly against them in our autumn match and were bent on revenge. And we won 2–1.

Then we met Juventus, the league leaders, and managed to win 1–0.

We had no problem finding the mental energy for these matches. We played with a knife at our throats in all three. But the team were not able to keep their concentration for the match against Valencia, which naturally was also very important for us – but not as decisive. The players had got it into their heads that the game would be easier, and were not as charged up as they were for the three previous matches. It was an away match and the return game was still to come if it didn't go that well – or so we thought.

As the coach, I should have had the courage in that situation to change several of our players. Not because they weren't good, but because I should have been able to foresee that a number of them wouldn't be able to keep up their concentration and create sufficient mental energy.

Railo:

That is a correct analysis. It shows that a team can be highly charged in one match, but almost completely lacking in energy not long afterwards, due to mental pressures and an excess of tension.

We talked earlier abut how the concept of mental energy had gained in importance in sport and would continue to do so. The best sportsmen probably train as much as ever, physically speaking, so there is little difference there. Even an athlete in top physical condition can lose against one that is not, the reason being that many athletes do not get 100 per cent out of themselves. Instead, mental blocks, negative thoughts, misdirected emotions, incorrect mental tension and a lack of mental energy result in their being second, third, fourth best.

Mental energy is not really so very different from physical energy. Mental energy too must be built up, used properly and rebuilt. It is a necessary resource if we are to attain the best results. If we have not learnt to deal correctly with our mental tension and energy, hard physical training will not make much difference. We will not be able to utilise our capacity to the full.

It's also important not to waste our mental energy. Unfortunately, it's easy to use energy on things other than the performance in hand. How many sportsmen waste their energy due to excessive or long-lasting nervousness and insecurity?

> Long periods of nervousness reduce mental energy

Most of us will know how nervousness can drain our energy: when we are nervous we also become tired, and if we are nervous for long periods of time – hours, days, perhaps weeks – our energy will already have been used up when it's finally time to compete.

A footballer I once worked with had to seek medical advice because he would become unaccountably tired during matches.

He would be exhausted after only 15–20 minutes and had to be substituted, even though he had trained fully. No physical problems could be discovered. Then it was learnt that he would become extremely nervous before matches, often as early as the day before. He was so worried about losing his place in the team that he lost all his mental energy. After mental training he had no problem whatsoever in completing his matches.

Mental Energy – more and more important

There are a number of things that can reduce the mental energy of a player or team. Let us name a few:

TOO MUCH NOVELTY
Many players believe that they become more tired in away games than at home, which is often true. New environments can be energy-draining, not least when

compared to one's normal, safe home environment. If we take a good player from a small club who gets a contract with a big club such as Manchester United, Arsenal or Liverpool, he will be in danger of having less surplus energy in his new environment.

> Save your mental energy

One way of counteracting this is to create a 'feeling of home' in the new environment. Generally speaking, it's good to know as much as we can about the environment of a future competition: the stadium, the climate, the public, the hotel, the facilities. In this way, our energy can be used for what it has been built up for – performances on the sports field.

MONOTONY

Some kinds of training are characterised by monotony – another thing that uses up energy. A coach may have decided on a programme, forcing the person in his charge to follow it, regardless of how monotonous it might be.

Furthermore, to wander idly about is just one example of how energy can be wasted. This time the reason is a lack of stimulation.

CONFLICTS

Conflicts provide us with another example of the incorrect use of energy. Mental energy disappears in quarrels, whether through aggression or defence. It is therefore particularly important that coaches and other leaders work on nipping conflicts in the bud. They should go in and clear them up quickly.

> Conflicts kill mental energy

SOLEMNITY

Being too serious is yet another way of wasting energy. Some sportsmen actually believe that they will have a frivolous image unless they go around with a solemn face before an important match. Too little 'happy' nervousness and too much 'solemn' nervousness will destroy energy. We mentioned earlier that fun will improve a performance. The same thing applies to happy nervousness: happy nervousness produces energy. We will of course be nervous, but at the same time, dying to compete and just a bit impatient. Solemn nervousness costs energy. We may dread a competition, so we look solemn, are defensive in our thoughts and lack that spark when the referee blows his whistle for the kick-off.

Other things that sap the sportsman's energy are:

- Big time differences.
- Big differences in temperature.
- Long periods of nervousness.
- Insufficient encouragement.
- Insufficient support from the social environment.

Björn Borg trained his willpower

We can work systematically on our production of mental energy.

Imagine a football team's usual training session – a gloomy, grey Thursday evening in February. How much energy will the players be able to summon up for the session?

In practice, few will give everything they have – probably about 80 per cent, or even less. The problem is that, in the match the following weekend, the same players want to generate 100 per cent. This can be difficult. If we are accustomed to the 80 per cent level during training, it will be difficult to find 100 per cent under competition conditions. Our fundamental rule is therefore: 100 per cent in competition requires 100 per cent in training – on the mental plane, too.

Always train 100 per cent

This applies especially to two kinds of sport:

- Those that are physically demanding, such as football, cycling, running, skiing, and so on.
- Those that require long periods of concentration – such as tennis or golf.

We spoke about how Björn Borg worked on his willpower. This kind of training is also a kind of energy training.

There is great scope for improvement in this area. For many people, quantity comes before quality in training. Going instead for shorter spells of very high-quality intensity and concentration can enhance the ability to mobilise mental energy. Conversely, training for quantity can result in a failure to generate fully the mental energy we have the potential to produce.

This method also makes it possible to have essential rest between training spells – and that means mental rest, too.

Remember:

- Too little and too much mental tension is detrimental to performance.
- Too much tension will lead to mental blocking.
- Too little tension will sap energy.
- Learn to adjust tension yourself.
- Pressure, humour and motivation are positive creators of tension.
- Aggression is a negative creator of tension.
- Mental energy is built through 100 per cent quality during training.

There are many energy killers:

- Excessive and long-lasting nervousness.
- Too much novelty.
- Monotony.
- Conflicts.
- Solemnity.

SETTING GOALS

– Breaking through barriers

The Dutch ice-skater, Ard Schenk, was supreme in the world at the beginning of the 1970s and set a string of world records. Now imagine a woman skater competing against Schenk in one of his record runs – and skating faster. Impossible? Not at all. For this was just what happened – even though it took place 16 years later. In 1988 a number of female skaters bettered Schenk's world record in the 3,000 metres. This begs the question: would they have been able to do this as early as 1972?

Well, why not? If they had then been working with the right kind of goals, it would have been entirely possible.

> *Break through all the barriers*

Eriksson:
What do you mean by the right kind of goals?

Railo:
Everyone knows what a goal is. The point is that we have to differentiate between different kinds of goals. A goal is a 'mental projection of something we wish to achieve within a given period of time'. For example, to win *Lo Scudetto* within three years is a typical goal.

It is important to differentiate between a 'result' goal and a 'process' goal. Winning the league is a typical result goal. And it is in this way that we normally think of goals. But as far as I am concerned, a process goal is just as important – perhaps more so, as it shows the processes that must be overcome to achieve the result.

In football, it might be the measurement of strength, fitness, speed, and technical and tactical skills, which have to be learnt within a given period of time. Goals should furthermore be broken down for individual players. I believe that process goals nowadays are not concrete enough, which is why the systematic learning of them is so poor.

Eriksson:

It's true that we don't concentrate sufficiently on 'learning goals' during training sessions, and that we are not very good at following up individual players where these process goals are concerned.

Railo:

I have seen this when I have been in the changing room before training sessions and I've asked the players: 'What are you going to learn today? What are your concrete learning goals other than that you'll just go out and train?' And after training sessions, I have sometimes asked players to describe what they have learnt. The answers are nearly always vague.

> *'What did we actually learn today?'*

Thus, process goals are often vague, while result goals are very concrete. We could improve this in football.

Mats Wilander achieved his goal

In addition to result goals and process goals, I think it's important to differentiate between:
- Security goals.
- Realistic goals
- Barrier-breaking goals.

We have to know how these different goals will affect performance because there are two dangers that exist in only working with 'realistic' goals:

FIRST DANGER:

As soon as the brain registers that a goal has been reached, or is very likely to be reached, our mental energy sinks. You can just imagine coming to the finishing line of the 10,000 metres. Just as you are about to cross the line, you hear your trainer shout: 'One more lap to go!'

> *Mental energy sinks at the finishing line*

Even if, physically speaking, we were able to do another lap, we all know that, mentally, we wouldn't be up to it. Research has also been done in this area. Athletes loaded down with lead are asked to run 40 and 60 metres with their loads. When they are asked to run 40 metres, they are to report at what time during the run they feel so heavy that they want to give up.

The average answer to this is when 80 per cent of the run has been completed. When the distance is now increased and the goal set to 60 metres, the feeling of wanting to give up also comes at 80 per cent of the run. The explanation is that feelings of tiredness are to a large extent dependent on the concrete goal that athletes have been led to expect.

Another example from sport is when the following goal is set: 'We're going to get to the final.' It so often happens that once the final is reached, the brain will unconsciously register that the goal has been attained. And energy will sink.

> *'I can't do any more now'*

The conscious will only partially compensate for the unconscious feeling of having reached the goal.

Railo:

The most extreme example of this, which I myself have worked with, is that of Mats Wilander, the Swedish tennis player. He had already, as a little boy, set himself the goal of being the world's number one in tennis and for many years his mind occupied itself with that projection. So what were the consequences when he in fact became number one?

Well, his mental energy sank dramatically. Even if he wanted to continue playing among the world's élite, his ability to win had been compromised.

What is interesting here is that a conflict ensued in which his conscious mind said, 'I want to continue playing tennis,' and his subconscious said, 'Sorry Mats, game over!' The unconscious feeling of reaching a goal almost always wins over the conscious will.

Another example is the match between France and Italy in the final of the 2000 European Championship. Italy were leading France 1–0 with only 50 seconds of the match remaining. This scoreline was astonishing for most people as France were the favourites. But with only 50 seconds remaining, Italy had not only 'reached' their goal, they had exceeded it. This led to a feeling, whether conscious or unconscious, of having crossed the finishing line, which in turn resulted in the players' energy sinking so low that France were able to get a shot in. France equalised and forced extra time against a by now enfeebled Italian side. They duly went on to win the game.

This is just an example of what a premature feeling of attaining one's goal can lead to. Furthermore, it is interesting to note that, in a later interview, Paolo Maldini said that the Italian team had felt that if the match went into extra-time, France would win – which is exactly what they did.

SECOND DANGER:

There is another thing that is even more important than simply working with realistic goals:

if the realistic goal is set too low, it can function as a barrier and actually will be more negative than positive.

Goals as mental barriers .

Railo:

As I mentioned earlier, I worked with Ingrid Kristiansen, who set three world records in 1986: the 5,000 metres, 10,000 metres and the marathon. She had come to me two years earlier after a really poor effort in the 1984 Los Angeles Olympics. My first question to her was: 'How fast do you think women will be running the 10,000 metres in seven years?'

The times that Ingrid indicated were far better than the world record then.

My next question was: 'What new training methods do you think will have come to light in seven years?'

She replied that so much was known about medicine in sport that it was improbable that anything new would be in use, though there might possibly be more altitude training.

My last question was: 'Why should you wait for seven years to run these times?' Thus, I suggested that she should run the new times in two years, not seven. In order to achieve this, we had to have at least two goals: one realistic and another that was barrier-breaking.

We began training with different barrier-breaking projections, which Ingrid used both at home with her mental training and during her physical training. In the end, her mind was programmed with projections including new world record times. Two years later she set three world records, which was considered to be sensational at the time.

Barrier-breaking goal: win the league

Eriksson:

I also followed this principle with Lazio. As I have said, the club hadn't won anything particular for 26 years. We were obliged to begin to work with the idea that Lazio would in fact be able to win the Italian League. But it took time to get the players to accept that they didn't necessarily have to finish after Milan and Juventus. And in 2000 we won *Lo Scudetto*.

Railo:

It just goes to show how very important it is to work with barrier-breaking goals.

It's not a good idea to set a goal at just one level. As I said, the realistic goal can end up having a braking effect once it has been reached.

Barrier-breaking goals, on the other hand, can function as ice-breakers: they penetrate through subconscious blocking mechanisms and draw the person to yet greater heights.

> *Goals with freedom and enjoyment – never demands*

We must connect feelings of joy, freedom and opportunity to barrier-breaking goals, but never demands or obligations. It should never feel like a failure or disappointment if we do not reach a goal. The main function of a barrier-breaking goal is to prepare the subconscious for the idea that we want to go further than we previously thought was possible. The physical boundary often lies much further away than the psychological one – another argument for barrier-breaking goals.

The mind needs time to work with barrier-breaking projections. Short-term, dreamy thoughts are not enough. The mind requires a long time with constant repetitions to accept these projections deeply and unconsciously. Mental pictures have to be fully accepted if they are to have real power.

> ## The mind needs barrier-breaking images

This is most easily shown using a high jumper as an example. Suppose that we have a high jumper who often clears 2.30 metres and sometimes 2.33. What would his goal look like? Well, a conventional trainer would probably go right ahead with 2.40, but we would set the following goals in accordance with the model we have just described:

- A security goal of 2.30. This is rather on the low side, given his current capability, but still must be judged to be a clearly acceptable result.
- A realistic, 'jobbing' goal of 2.36. This is still a bit from the height he has cleared so far, but should not feel at all impossible.
- A barrier-breaking goal of, say, 2.42.

Eriksson:

I know what you mean. The Swedish national side did not have a goal that was sufficiently barrier-breaking during the 1992 European Championships at home, when they came to a halt in the semi-finals. The team did have the ability to go further, based on experience of various tournaments.

And one could well ask what happened to my former team, Lazio, in the summer of 1999. We led in the league by five or six points, after a long string of victories, but then lost it all in the end. We probably became self-satisfied and thought we had already reached our goal.

> ## Goals must be concrete, not vague

Railo:

We can see the same thing happening when a team, or an individual sportsman, causes a surprise in a tournament. Even if they get to the final, they seldom win. They are happy just to have reached the final and can't find the requisite mental energy and motivation. The mind has unconsciously registered that the goal has been reached. The energy can certainly be built up again, but it takes time. It is desirable to have barrier-breaking goals at this point too, as they give protection against this unconscious feeling of having reached one's goal.

Effective goals – what is required?

Let us now go through our 'table of requirements' for goals:

- **Goals must be concrete.** Vaguely expressed goals of the 'we must improve' kind carry no pulling power.

  Very often sportsmen will say: 'I'll do my best – then we'll see how far that goes.' If this constitutes the whole goal-setting process, it's not going to pay very high dividends.

- **Goals should be consciously accepted by all those who are to attain them.** This can sound obvious, but how often does one see that players and coaches have different ideas about what the goals should actually be in training and in competition.

- **Goals must be connected to the daily grind.** The point about this is that we should know whether we are on the right course for our 'mental projection'. It is important to have a constant, direct connection with our everyday life. And now we're talking about technique, tactics, behaviour and results.

- **A goal must be sufficiently high.** This might sound obvious too. Can a goal ever be too high? The answer is yes. If he tries to make use of a goal that's unrealistically high, the athlete will, consciously or unconsciously, defend himself against it. But a goal mustn't be too low either or there won't be any pulling power to it. It may then function as a barrier or 'dream' limit. That's why we recommended the combination of 'realistic' and 'barrier-breaking' goals.

- **Goals must be anchored in self-confidence,** otherwise they risk just becoming something we want to defend ourselves against – or something that lowers our self-confidence. Setting up goals that have no solid relation to our, or our team's, self-confidence is really dangerous. Working with goals means as much as working with self-confidence.

> *Goals and self-confidence go together*

- **Goals must be accepted mentally and accepted completely,** otherwise there is a definite risk of a mental protest reaction or block. We could be somewhat provocative and say that the problem is not setting up the goal – it's getting it accepted mentally.

  Goal acceptance can be described as a process involving four steps:

  1. We don't accept the goal at all. As we have said, the goal will instead become something that we must defend ourselves against. We become mentally defensive.

  2. We accept the goal intellectually but not emotionally. A team's players might say: 'Of course we're going to beat Arsenal in the cup.' But deep down they know that this is impossible.

  3. We accept the goal both intellectually and emotionally, but only consciously. The braking signals from your subconscious are still there.

  We thus differentiate between conscious and unconscious goals. We have outlined the process of setting a conscious goal. A subconscious goal is one that our brain, deep down, accepts. If a connection is missing between these two types of goal, you can bet your bottom dollar that it is the unconscious goal which will dominate. As we mentioned earlier, it is terribly important that goals are accepted – and that means the subconscious too.

4. We fully accept a goal, both consciously and subconsciously deep down. Our goal then becomes a part of us, not simply something that we have 'set up'.

- **Goals must be learnt systematically.** And so they must be shaped in a certain way. Here, in combination, is the best way:

  'I'm going to score nine goals next season.'

  'I can see images where I really score nine goals next season.'

  'I really feel, deep inside, that I can score nine goals next season.'

  Working with these three expressions in combination gives the best results.

Remember:

- Goals must be concrete, measurable and personal.
- There must be goals both for the result and for the processes that culminate with the result.
- We never know what we can realistically attain, so work with what you think is a realistic goal, and add a barrier-breaking goal.
- Barrier-breaking goals must never be associated with force or disappointment.
- Always associate joy and freedom with your barrier-breaking goals.
- The concept of a goal exists both at the conscious and the subconscious level – but it is always the subconscious that wins.
- A goal projection will not have a major effect until it is accepted emotionally and subconsciously.
- Goals and self-confidence must go hand in hand.

THE POWER OF THE MIND

– How our mind governs our performance

Eriksson:

When I was coach at Roma I had a player the whole team was very dependent on: Falcao, from Brazil. Due to an injury (connected with cartilage building in the knee), he only had four matches with us during my time at the club. But in the matches he played, Roma were a completely different team. He went around the pitch, pointing and co-ordinating.

When he wasn't able to play, players would come to me and say:

'We can't play without Falcao.'

That season we came sixth in the league. The following year, with just about the same team, we came second and won the cup. But it took me a whole year to get the players to understand that we could also play without Falcao. Without him, the players suffered a block. Falcao's presence or absence was decisive in determining how the players felt, and this in turn determined how well they played.

Powerful thoughts

Railo:

It is a well-known phenomenon that our mind can dominate in determining our behaviour, whether positively or negatively. The most dramatic example of this is death by voodoo, where it is actually possible for a person to 'think himself into' his own death.

> Our thoughts can make us ill – and well

Another well-known example is how our thinking can affect our health – especially with illnesses linked to the immune system. In medicine, the placebo effect has been known for many years. The idea is that if we believe we are going to be ill, we can in fact be ill. Similarly, if we are ill but believe we can be well, we can get better – or even be completely cured of our illness.

I myself have worked with athletes who think themselves into illness, or poor form. I have also worked with those who are able to think themselves back to good health and good form.

We can also look at some simple examples from ordinary everyday life of which many people will have some experience:

'Feel that you're falling backwards'

Stand with your back about 10–15 cm from a wall. Shut your eyes, relax and think to yourself: 'I'm falling backwards, I'm falling backwards, I'm falling backwards...' Note how your muscles react. Although you have not given them any orders, they tense up and you begin to fight to control your balance – and 90 per cent of the time you also fall backwards.

As part of their mental training, I took a few athletes to a hospital to measure their brain activity by means of an EEG. After concentrating for only a few minutes on relaxing, the tension in their brains went down dramatically. But as soon as they imagined themselves in a competition or a match, their brain activity increased just as dramatically.

In sport, it is customary to focus on the physical body, on what happens to our arms and legs. Coaches and sportsmen are accustomed to looking at what went wrong and subsequently trying to work harder on different muscle groups and improving technique or tactics. But very few are interested in the dominating mental impulses which form the basis of everything, and so no distinction is made between what we can see directly, the symptom, and the underlying cause, which is what in reality governs our performance.

Our mind governs our body

The power of the mind is, in many ways, simply fantastic. However, we should remember that the mind governs consciously, as well as subconsciously. When a sportsman wins because he 'wanted it most', a conscious decision has been involved, one that he made on the level of his willpower. Here we are going to look at the power of the subconscious mind. If our mind is prompted with the right thoughts from our subconscious, we will be in a position to do things that no one would have thought possible – not even ourselves.

The problem for many sportsmen is often that the mind's power, far from helping them, confuses them. Instead of producing accelerating power, their thoughts function as a brake because of the direction they have taken and the way this in turn affects performance. Let us suppose that we face a challenge: a difficult match, a tough competition, a spell which increases our mental tension. There will be different ways of reacting:

• We can think 'fight or flight'.
• We can think 'attack or defence'.
• We can think 'freedom or compulsion'.

These are just a few examples of how we can think. We'll be looking at this more closely in the chapter on mental training.

Plus and minus

Our mind can vacillate between positive and negative impulses. By positive impulses, we mean thoughts, feelings and energy that govern us positively.

Negative impulses are the opposite: thoughts, feelings and mental energy that govern us negatively. The point here is obviously to change our negative impulses so that they stimulate us positively.

Eriksson:

If I have understood correctly, there are factors which are typical of a 'plus' mind.

Railo:

That's right. Here are some characteristics:

- Be eager but not tense.
- Be self-confident but not conceited.
- Think positively, even in adversity.
- Feel secure in yourself and in your team.
- Feel joyful and free.
- Think offensively, even when technically defending yourself.
- Have an inner conviction of your goal, and low performance anxiety.

Do this simple little test: close your eyes, relax and conjure up a picture of yourself in a situation when you were successful. Now write down the thoughts and feelings you associate with this situation. Then do exactly the opposite. Conjure up a mental picture of an instance of failure, noting down what you thought and felt then.

This will give you some idea of your 'plus' mind and your 'minus' mind.

Fight or flight

On the basis of the plus mind and the minus mind, let's now see how we can react in different situations.

> 'How can I avoid getting the ball?'

An example:

An important international cup match between two international teams goes into extra-time – and then penalties. At the same time as the referee blows his whistle to end extra time, one of the most experienced players in the away team limps off the field with a feigned injury. Now one of the youngest players in the team will have to take a penalty. Of course, with 50,000 fans whistling and booing in the stands, the task is too much for him: the young player strikes his penalty kick high over the crossbar.

The action of the experienced player is a clear example of flight prevailing over fight.

> Flight under pressure

In this critical situation, the experienced player would of course have had masses of mental energy, which he could have used in two ways. He could have said to himself: 'This is going to be tough, this is going to be difficult, but it is also stimulating and challenging. I know I can take the pressure. I'll convert the penalty!'

But he went the other way: 'Oh, this really is too tough, this is too difficult, I can't handle this. I'm off!'

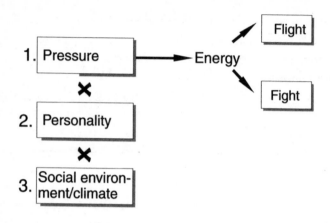

Railo:

We choose, consciously or subconsciously, how we are to direct our mental energy.

1. WE CAN DIRECT OUR ENERGY INTO 'FIGHT'.

A typical 'fight' reaction is to think offensively, dare to take risks, venture to keep motivation high and keep our goal in mind. All our energy is directed to the task itself.

2. WE CAN DIRECT OUR ENERGY INTO 'FLIGHT'.

We can devote a lot of mental energy to ourselves and our inner defence. Obviously, less energy is going to go into the performance itself. It can generally be said that the greater the mental tension, the greater the danger that individual players, even an entire team, will react with flight.

> *Aggression is usually flight*

In addition, aggression is often flight in disguise and not a fighting reaction, as many people might think. Our example of the footballer who didn't want to take the important penalty illustrates something that we will call 'stress-flight'. In certain exposed situations, we can all suffer from it.

But there is also something that we can call 'habitual flight', where a sportsman or a whole team has accepted the behaviour of flight. Flight then becomes an attitude: we give up in advance. Oddly enough, it is often easier to change habitual flight than stress flight. A coach who breaks bad habits in the right way can turn flight into fight.

Railo:

When I'm lecturing I sometimes introduce a competition based on mental arithmetic. I divide the public into two opposing teams and emphasise before the competition that we're going to be using elementary arithmetic. The only thing I require is that everything should be quick – and correct.

I tell them that not everyone can be in the competition and so I want to select representatives from each team.

You can clearly see the fight-flight reactions as representatives are being selected. Many people begin to think: 'How can I get out of this?' One guy once got up and explained that he had forgotten an important meeting he had to get to. Unfortunately, few people take the 'fight' option and think: 'Right, this is going to be fun. Let's get going – then we'll see who's a dummy!'

Typical 'flight' reactions are:

- We become defensive and evasive.
- Our self-confidence sinks.
- Setting of goals goes out the window.
- We become enfeebled and feel apathetic.
- Our concentration goes down.
- We stop taking risks.
- We delegate responsibility.
- We overestimate our opponents.
- The air is thick with excuses.

> Play defensively but be offensive mentally

This is quite typical in the world of sport. When the pressure increases, so does the danger of flight behaviour and poor results.

> When the pressure rises, so does the danger of flight

One way of noting flight behaviour is to listen to the excuses. Let's look at some of them:

'I haven't been training well lately.'

'The ref's against us.'

'I'm injured, actually.'

'The crowd here is terrible.'

'The changing-rooms are sub-standard.'

'How can you play in this stadium?'

'The pitch is too dry.'

'The grass is too wet.'

We see, too, how some players lie on the grass writhing in pain after receiving the lightest of knocks. To leave the field limping while a replacement is sent on is a convenient way to flee – instead of staying to fight.

Some players can be heard setting their sights on victory a couple of weeks before an important competition. But the closer the day of the competition, the lower their sights get. One week before the competition, the goal has now changed to reaching the final, not to winning. The day before the competition, one player says that he will be happy just to have taken part.

Eriksson:

I know the players who usually develop an injury in the training session before an important match. They are usually the most nervous and anxious ones. They try to escape from reality with imaginary injuries. It's pointless to include these types of players in your team. I've gradually got to know the ones that pretend – and the ones who are genuinely injured. The physio has a special role in all teams. Perhaps because it's his job to have such a physical contact with the players that his position is so unique. If only the coach could hear everything that was said between the physio and the players. My ideal would be to have a physio who was a psychologist.

Railo:

I have several examples of a flight reaction with footballers I've worked with.

> Players can believe they are ill

One player would turn up full of fight at training sessions and for ordinary matches. But as soon as there was an important match – an international, a cup final, a crucial league match – he would become hesitant and his shots would lack power. When we talked about it, he explained that in these important matches he actually felt physically weak, even small. So he wanted to flee. We were able to put this right with mental training.

Another player had feelings of doubt and hesitancy, the result of a flight reaction. He was afraid to meet the defenders when he approached the opposite goal. He told me afterwards that he was happy just to get past one of the defenders and then his job would be done. So he didn't bother to get within shooting range.

A third player had roughly the same problem as the first. The main thing on his mind in important matches was to pass the ball to his team-mates as quickly as possible, so that he was released from all responsibility.

Another player was even worse – he would 'hide' on the field so that he wouldn't have to play the ball at all. Then there was no risk of making a fool of himself.

Naturally, there are many factors that make us react as we do. Let us quickly look at some of them:

PERSONALITY

Two players of otherwise equal ability will produce entirely different results because the personality of one is inclined to flight, while that of the other is to fight.

Some can tolerate very little tension before they are put to flight, while others react to increased pressure and tension by continuing to fight.

SOCIAL ENVIRONMENT

If a team has an inner solidarity, the players will find it very much easier to respond with a fighting attitude, for they feel secure. Everybody works for each other, everybody supports everybody else. IFK Gothenburg won the 1982 UEFA Cup. In the final against Hamburg at the Volkparks stadium, one of the key Swedish players was injured early in the match. But the IFK Gothenburg players responded aggressively to increasing mental tension – and won 3–0.

WAY OF THINKING

Two teams with exactly the same ability, exposed to exactly the same mental pressure, will have different results due to the teams' way of thinking. By learning to think in terms of offence, individual players and the whole team can develop a way of thinking which will come in very useful when they are exposed to pressure.

Eriksson:

There are many examples of how players are negatively affected when their social environment lets them down.

> When our social environment lets us down

When I was coach at Benfica (1982–84), we had a player who was certainly one of the best in Europe. He was not only a fantastic player and team member, he also had a great personality. He got a new girlfriend and suddenly everything changed. She had to be at all the training sessions, on trips, at the hotel – in the end even on the bench during our matches. Naturally, those were demands I couldn't accept.

In the end, this player was sold to a foreign club, and the same story was repeated there. He was allowed to keep his contract but was dropped from the team and didn't play any more matches. His career ended when he was only 25 or 26.

Railo:

Do you think that players and coaches think of 'fight' and aggression as more or less the same thing?

Eriksson:

There are probably many that do, unfortunately. For me, these are two different things entirely. I see aggression as a 'flight' reaction. We feel so much pressure that we respond in panic. Aggression is based on insecurity. Real fighting spirit is based on inner security and self-confidence.

> *Americans meet difficulties head on*

I'm inclined to think sometimes that American sportsmen are better at fighting. That's one of the positive things about the American believe-in-yourself culture: the courage to meet difficulties head-on and overcome adversity. Fred Shero, the legendary coach of the New York Rangers had a maxim which has become something of a catchphrase now: 'When the going gets tough, the tough get going.'

That's something we could all take to the next match.

Typical 'fight' reactions are:

• We are offensive and get stuck into the job (without aggression).

- We keep our goal uppermost in our mind.
- Motivation is constantly high.
- Energy is used to attack, and not defend.
- We have belief in our own ability.

Attack or defence

Eriksson:

I've noticed that when I place a defence further forward on the field the players are more inclined to attack. If I have the same type of play further back, the players assume a more defensive way of thinking, although the same play and the same tactics are actually involved. All I've done is move the position of play on the field, yet the players seem to react defensively – and then their game often suffers. What do you think?

Railo:

You're quite right. I differentiate between the 'attacking mind' and the 'defensive mind'. We know that the attacking mind, which means that we are offensive but not aggressive, almost always produces better results.

> *An attacking mind produces results*

What you have described can often be seen in teams who take the lead in a match – and then try to defend it. When the coach switches to more defensive tactics, the players also begin to think defensively. They were effective in attack when the score was still 0–0, but now that they are playing to hang on to the lead they are unable to play positively. Instead, they only think in defensive terms.

Note that I'm talking here about having an attacking mentality, not about actually playing offensively or defensively, or whatever the tactics might be. To think in terms of defence or attack is not quite the same thing as 'flight' or 'fight'.

Fight or flight is an emotional way of reacting. Attack or defence is a way of thinking that we adopt. An attacking way of thinking has great importance. It is partly determined by our personality: some people are born with an attacking will. We should emphasise here the importance of training and the general attitude to matches regardless of how important they are. Our will also requires training, in the same way as everything else. The way we tackle a setback is very important. The foundation for winning often lies in a loss and the way we deal with that loss. Defensive thinking after a loss will only produce a negative basis for future matches.

Björn Borg had ten basic rules in training

Let us also look at an example of the importance of training – and how we can also think offensively even when we don't feel like it. Björn Borg had ten basic rules in his training. Several of these were about having a strong will and thinking offensively.

Borg once told me how he never missed a training session, regardless of whether he felt like training, or it was raining or for whatever reason. Instead, he would use the session to train his will. For him, 'will' meant the ability to resist and triumph over adversity. When everything is against us and nothing goes right, when our mind has a heavy weight to carry – that's when we need our will. In this way, Borg used setbacks and his reluctance to train to develop an attacking will that he could use to do his utmost in matches. Training his willpower became purely routine for him.

I wonder whether this is familiar to you? Have you had players who always thought positively in terms of offence rather than defence?

Eriksson:

I have had many such players like that over the years but there is one that comes to mind now, one I have mentioned before – Mihajlovic. When a match hots up, he can turn it around through his brilliant technique, but perhaps even more, through his attacking approach. He's almost like a traffic policeman out there, directing everything, with the other players responding to his play. His willpower seems to spread to the rest of the team. Other players that I could mention in this connection are Nesta, Vieri and Simeone. They have this fantastic ability to take the team with them in a positive direction when the going gets tough. Their playing strength and competitive spirit are both very impressive.

> *One player's willpower can spread across the team*

Railo:

I can give you a very good example of the difference between the defensive mind and the attacking mind. Two equally good cyclists are to compete in a velodrome, but they have prepared in completely different ways.

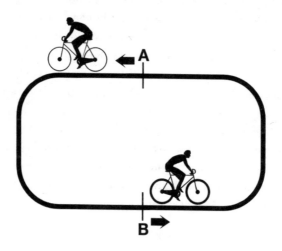

Cyclist A thinks: 'I'm going to do my utmost to catch up with B.'

Cyclist B thinks: 'I'm going to do my utmost to keep A behind me.'

A is thus thinking about attacking, while B is doing his best to defend himself.

Which one of the cyclists do you think proved to be best? The result was exactly as we would expect. The cyclist who was prepared to think in terms of attack had better times than the one who only wanted to defend himself.

We should point out again, however, that this only refers to our mental orientation, and not tactics. We have to be careful to differentiate between defensive and offensive tactics and defensive and offensive spirit. Some teams in fact always do best as underdogs, when they have everything to win and nothing to lose, in which case they play with defensive tactics but with offensive thinking, an 'attacking' mind.

Let the mind come before the performance

The mind normally engages after the performance, but I believe we should have the opposite: first engage the mind and open the door for the performance. I believe that matches and results play far too large a part in a player's own mental performance. The opposite is actually more desirable: we should train hard mentally so that the mind continually elicits performances, regardless of results in an individual competition or match, otherwise we can become focused on tenths of a second, or centimetres, or scores.

It is clear that sportsmen train too little mentally, limiting the exercise of their mental strength by only allowing it to function in terms of results.

If things go well we become mentally strong, but when there's a setback we give in too easily. Remember that it is in adversity that the mind and the will are trained. It is in adversity that we lay the foundations for success.

> *The mind is trained best in adversity*

Freedom or compulsion?

Think about the following sentences:

'I must, I should, I've got to.'

'I want to, I'll have a go, I can.'

It is fairly natural that we will not perform as well if we are forced to do something rather than being free to do the same thing. It is also true that many sportsmen feel an unexpressed compulsion from their environment to reach certain goals. A typical example of the wrong type of thinking is the thought 'Now I mustn't miss'.

Try this little exercise. Close your eyes, relax and imagine you are in a competition or match that's coming up. You see yourself on the track or pitch and you think 'I must, I should, I've got to'.

How do you feel? Don't you feel that your personality withers, your mood sinks, your desire fades? After a moment or two, repeat the exercise, but think instead 'I want to, I'll have a go, I can'. Now you immediately feel better. You're practically raring to go.

> *'I feel free'*

One of the world's top skaters, Tomas Gustafson, won three Olympic gold medals in his career. Since competing could be long and monotonous (his distances were the 5,000 and 10,000 metres), a lot of thoughts had time to go through his head. But, as Gustafson said himself, 'Out on the ice, I felt this great feeling of freedom. It was just me against the clock.'

Tomas Gustafson had been training mentally for a long time and had used this both to recharge his batteries and to relax. Outside pressure is hard to change, but we can create a feeling of freedom by choosing how we think – and mentally train.

Remember:

- Our thoughts govern our performance, both now and in the long term.
- The power of the mind affects feelings, performances and mental energy.
- Our thoughts control us, both consciously and subconsciously.
- A thought we think today is stored by the brain and determines our actions tomorrow, subconsciously.
- We are the sum of what we have thought during our life.
- Mental training is the conscious and active management of positive thoughts and mental images, with reference to concrete situations.
- Previous negative thinking can be changed to positive thinking by thinking afresh.
- Work up your plus mind, eliminate your minus mind.
- An attacking mentality gives better results than a defensive mentality.
- Aggression is often an indication of flight.
- Excuses are a manifestation of flight behaviour.
- 'Fight' or 'flight' attitudes depend on our personality and social environment.
- The will also requires training.
- Our mind should engage before a performance – not the other way round.
- Think 'I want to, I'll have a go, I can', instead of 'I must, I should, I've got to'.

THE GOOD TEAM

– The culture of winning and the coach's role

Two teams with big reputations, Milan and Juventus, have remarkably high standards in their mental approach. For a long time now they have looked on victory as their birthright, and positive thinking dominates in these clubs. Of course, one reason for this is the success they have had, but a winning culture can also be created.

Railo:

A winning culture is promoted by rewarding and 'punishing' behaviour, so that we adapt to desired values, norms and attitudes. The individual quickly adapts to the group's routines, habits, conditions, values and use of language. The base of a culture is its collective mentality, what we can call its 'mental culture'.

The mental culture in a group of people – be it a family, a football team, a company, or a nation – cannot be underestimated. We have already shown that the way we think is crucial to our personal success. The same thing goes for whole teams, clubs, sometimes whole sports.

How do we think collectively?

Eriksson:

Two years ago, nobody in Lazio believed that the club would be able to win the league. It hadn't happened in 26 years. Lazio had developed a culture in which people thought in terms of 'bad luck'. As soon as anything happened to confirm this, people said: 'Typical Lazio...'

Railo:

It is important to understand how to build a culture which can defeat adversity and do the unexpected, the theoretically impossible. To begin with, we can say that culture is produced by the spread and acceptance of thoughts. A team's mental culture will set the pattern for how the players and the team react in different situations.

> *Be proud when you put on the team shirt*

Eriksson:

Yes, it's important to be proud when you put on your team shirt. In a winning culture people think 'We're good, we have nothing to be afraid of. We're not bothered by what the opposition can do. We do our own thing'.

Railo:

One problem is that negative thinking spreads more quickly than positive thinking. If a player in a team thinks negatively, he can easily infect another player. And if two think negatively, soon it will be four. In no time at all the whole team will have a negative mental culture, a losing culture. Players then see the difficulties on the field, seldom the possibilities. I have seen many examples of players who have come to negative cultures and been destroyed.

> *Negative thoughts spread more quickly than positive ones*

But the opposite also applies: players who come to a positive mental culture themselves begin to think in positive ways. This will give better performances – something that makes us think still more positively – and then we have a winning culture in the team.

Building a winning team

We can look at two teams with completely different mental cultures:

In team A, the following thoughts dominate:

'Don't set your goals so high that you can't reach them.'

'We're too small to hold our own internationally.'

'We must, we should, we're going to.'

'Too much responsibility can be tough.'

'How come everybody else has better terms than us?'

In team B, there is the following mental culture:

'It's exciting to shoulder the responsibility.'

'We support each other in all respects.'

'Changes are exciting.'

'We want to, we'll have a go, we can.'

'We keep to our goals, even when there's a setback.'

'We attack, regardless of the situation.'

Obviously, team B is going to have the greater success. Let us briefly characterise a winning culture. The following will dominate:

- Barrier-breaking goals.
- Visionary thinking.
- A strong 'we' feeling.
- Offensive thinking.
- Great self-confidence.
- High mental level.
- Low performance anxiety.
- Wide security zone.
- Fresh thinking.
- The involvement of everyone, with each person equally important.
- Concentration on quality in all situations.

Railo:

There are essentially two ways of building a winning culture:

1. A GOOD EXAMPLE

A sportsman shows the way forward and becomes a good example for others.

Swedish tennis was for a long time at a low ebb internationally, until Björn Borg won Wimbledon.

Suddenly, a little country with only nine million inhabitants began to produce one world-class player after the other, such as Mats Wilander and Stefan Edberg. Conditions in Sweden had not changed: the cold climate and lack of indoor courts was as compromising as it had always been. But Borg had created the conditions for a winning culture in Swedish tennis.

> *Björn Borg – a good example*

He broke barriers, showed the way and became a good example for many others to follow. In addition, there were good leaders and coaches who understood how to make the most of Borg's barrier-breaking efforts, building cultures where talent could flourish.

Another Swedish star was Gunde Svan in long-distance skiing. He was a barrier-breaking example in his sport – but his successes did not have the same impact on the country as a whole.

Gunde explains this as follows: 'My thinking was very much "Gunde Svan". I had more than enough to do with taking care of myself, training and winning competitions. The problem was that everybody around me was also thinking "Gunde Svan". This may have been good for me but it did little to spread the word about the sport.'

So it's not enough to simply show the way forward. Leaders and coaches must also make the most of a good example.

The example method is good, but risky. Waiting for a role model to come along may take a long time. And then it's often too late.

2. DON'T WAIT – DO IT YOURSELF

Coaches can build winning cultures through their leadership. This path is built on analysis: which mental culture is dominant? What is positive? What is negative? We thus define the culture we want and begin to work systematically by steering others towards the desired culture.

The 'steering' approach is preferable as our principal method. If a winning culture is built first, both the group and, not least, the environment will accept success more readily. The role of the coach is crucial if this method is to succeed. He must be a barrier-breaking role model who dares to take the lead, taking the entire team with him in a spirit of winning.

> *A winning mentality must be encouraged by leading*

How did this work at Lazio? Did you trust in a good example, or did you choose to promote a culture?

Eriksson:

I combined the two methods you have described. An important strategy was to get new players who brought a winning attitude into the team. It was enough to have two or three players who could serve as my instrument when I wanted to change attitudes and the thinking in the team. I also made sure that there was a positive organisation around the team, so that everything ran smoothly and any unnecessary irritation could be avoided.

I already mentioned the Lazio phenomenon, which typically had it that we were an unlucky side. I changed this negative way of thinking and tried to stop players who represented the old culture from having an influence on the team.

I have also spoken a lot about the problems of lower division sides, who don't get much publicity from the press. Where referees are concerned, any 'help' is usually of the negative sort. But neither should you try to influence the referee. You have to think about how you can solve the problem yourself or you are well on the road to building a stock of alibis for when you lose – and this can be hard to overcome.

My job has often been to get teams to think of themselves as winners, so that they both see themselves as winners and feel that the outside world expects them to be, or become, winners. Once you get people to work towards the same goal, unbelievable things can happen. However, I would also like to emphasise that three things are necessary to create a winning culture:

1. Time
2. Clear short- and long-term goals.
3. Continuity and perseverance.

Short-term successes are, unfortunately, nearly always more important than these factors. If success is slow in coming, the pressure from outside is often so great that there's a revolution: the coach, style of play, and five or six players will be changed. There is then the danger of nullifying all the effort which has gone into building a winning culture, with one's sights on the long-term.

The Good Team

There is a popular notion of the loner winning against the odds. We would like to question that. We believe in 'together we stand'. But we also believe that it only takes one player to start to think negatively for others to start thinking in the same way. A bad atmosphere can spread quickly, particularly if one of the 'leaders of opinion' in the team represents the negative thinking – the captain, for instance.

The creation of team spirit and the building of 'the good team' is therefore one of the coach's most important jobs.

Let us together try to describe what is important in the creation of the good team. We have these eight points:

1. The good team has a common vision – a barrier-breaking mental projection which shows where the team wants to get.

2. The good team has clear and definite goals which go hand in hand with this vision. Goals must be the same for all, and be completely accepted by everyone – emotionally as well. Everyone in the team must, deep down, believe in their goals. We often find players who say that their goal is to win the league, for example, but at the same time feel that it's not really going to happen, that it's too unrealistic or ambitious. It is important in this situation that a coach makes sure that all the players have completely accepted the team's goals. Otherwise they won't be daring to win, not deeply and truly.

3. The good team's members share their understanding of strategy and tactics. This means both the general strategy, or the team's system of play, and the tactics in each individual match. Strategy must be hammered home during training sessions so that the players not only acknowledge it in words but can also demonstrate it under pressure.

4. The good team has great inner discipline. It should be clear how the players are to behave towards each other – and what the team rules are. These may cover time-keeping, mutual respect, helping other team-mates with problems and not achieving success at the cost of others. We often see how 'prima donnas' break the rules, something that can create unhappiness in a team. We know that team spirit will vanish when players begin to abuse each other and the internal level of criticism rises. It is imperative for the coach to intervene immediately – before morale goes.

5. The good team has players with characteristics which complement one another. A player like Ronaldo is a heaven-sent gift for a team – but it might not help to have four others like him. One Ronaldo is enough – the trick is to find other players, who can complement his gifts. A team should also include different personalities who can make contributions. Everything from the orderly types to the jokers, the lone wolves and the sociable guys, offensive and defensive. It can be hard to find the correct mix. We can say though, that it's not enough to simply take the best players in the belief that they will produce the best team.

6. The good team has a good division of roles among the players. Some take leading roles and others secondary roles because the fact is that some are natural leaders while others feel best when they don't have to adopt a leader's role. In this respect, the coach

must work to see that all members of his team are treated equally, even if their roles are different. There is always a danger that players with the most attractive roles will look down on others – and end up playing below their best. Intervention is necessary to stop some players growing at the cost of others. A true leader will not do that but instead will draw his team-mates with him to better performances. By contrast, prima donnas who delight in putting others down should be put on the bench. No one wins matches alone. Football is a team sport and everyone should realise this if they want a place in the good team. It is important to crack down on players who think their own interests can come before the interests of the other ten, thereby putting the whole team at risk.

7. The good team has players who put the common good before their own interests. In a way, all sportsmen are egoists, wanting to display their own ability. There's nothing wrong with that. It fosters a healthy ambition. But if personal success goes before the team's ability to play, the person concerned will find there's no future in it.

8. The good team has players who take responsibility for the whole team. Everyone thinks independently, but thinks 'we' rather than 'me' within the framework of the team. Everyone accepts mistakes as long as people do their best. Risks are encouraged, problems are things to be solved rather than obstacles, and everyone is free – but with responsibility.

Eriksson:

Let me give an example that illustrates how important it is to show confidence in players. When I was at Sampdoria we bought Platt from Juventus, and Gullit and Evani from Milan – three players who were thought to be past their best. But when they came to Sampdoria, all three blossomed again.

Sampdoria won the Italian Cup, reached the semi-finals of the Cup-Winners' Cup and had a cracking year in the league. We battled at the top until the end. The three players who were thought to be past it were as good as ever.

At the end of the year Milan bought back Gullit, but after only a few months of the autumn season he called me and said he wanted to come back. At Milan things hadn't gone as well as they had at Sampdoria.

But something had happened – Gullit had lost his motivation. He never found it again, not even when he returned to Sampdoria.

> *It is vital to show confidence in players*

The coach as mental builder

Earlier we emphasised the crucial role of the coach in building good team spirit and a winning culture. We believe that the coach, or leader, must take the initiative in this area.

It is coaches and leaders who must decide on the norms and values which are to guide the team or squad. This is not up for negotiation, although naturally a coach should listen to what his players have to say. A responsible coach who is deeply involved with a team does not begin to mess around with the values that he or she considers to be fundamental. Norms and values are hugely important to the thinking of players, and to the way in which the team's culture develops.

Earlier, we discussed how cultures could develop through different ways of thinking. The same applies to norms and values. In certain teams, nobody dares to take chances, everyone minds his own business and defeats turn into catastrophes. In other teams, everybody supports each other, is allowed to take the opportunity to develop and dares to take risks – even when there is a possibility of failure. Obviously, such different value systems will have an impact on team performances.

> *The coach as cultural architect*

We can differentiate between two kinds of coach: the one who goes down new paths and the one who sticks to the old ways. The coach of the future will:

- Break new ground to shape a new reality.
- Build winning cultures through being active and barrier-breaking.
- Show the way, produce a vision, create goals.
- Develop his team's level of energy – then direct this energy in the required direction.
- Identify future opportunities and create the conditions to try them.
- Work actively on self-confidence and mental culture.

Q and A

Railo:

I know that many readers would like to ask you a number of questions about your work as a coach. I put them to you now, on their behalf:

How do you select players for a team?

Eriksson:

The first condition, of course, is that they should be good players who fit in with our style of play. But, as I said before, I always like to have the right personality types. I like to have leaders. Leader figures have the advantage of being able to speak up. Football is also about communication. But I'd like to point out that you can be a good player without being a leader. You need both leader types and non-leaders to get a good team together.

When and why do you put a player on the bench?

Eriksson:

I always try to select the team that is best for the occasion, players who are in form.

But it also depends on the opposition. Which players would be best against Manchester United? Which should play against Reggina?

Do you put players on the bench as a punishment?

Eriksson:

I did sometimes as a young coach. I don't do it now – I would only be punishing myself. I have to make sure that I never select players who aren't in form, physically or mentally.

What makes you decide to make changes during matches?

Eriksson:

You can tell right away if a player is nervous, or somehow isn't being effective. Both from his game and his appearance, the player will be irritable and nervous. This may be caused by a number of things.

One factor could be that the opposition may have changed tactics and the player is unable to get into the match.

How far is it possible to control your tactics?

Eriksson:

We prepare ourselves having evaluated the opposition. We decide whether we are going to play 4–4–2 or 4–5–1, systems which the players are very familiar with and that we have practised again and again.

But is it possible to change tactics during the match itself?

Eriksson:

It's not easy, the reason being that it's difficult to get the information to everybody. Again, information can be misinterpreted when it has to go through several links.

Some players are also deaf to information when it comes during a match. They are so preoccupied with the play that they don't listen. In the end you might be left with only half the players understanding the change in tactics. Of course, it's easier to do it in the interval. I would love to be able to take a time-out in each half to talk to the players as a group.

---

some players are deaf to information in a match

Sometimes when a match turns, it seems that a few individual players have the power to change attitudes on the field. Have you had this experience?

Eriksson:

If I had to give an example of this, it would be Roberto Mancini, who played for both Sampdoria and Lazio. He could assess tactical changes during a match himself and had the ability to turn the game around. Your job as coach is easy when players are so good tactically.

It didn't hurt either that he was a footballing genius...

How did he influence the team?

Eriksson:

I can only say that he was a natural leader in a very characteristic sort of way. Lazio also had other natural leaders. I have already mentioned Mihajlovic and Veron from Argentina. Veron was the guy everybody wanted to play the ball to.

How did you select the team's captain?

Fan-tastic: Never in their wildest dreams did England fans expect the result of England's match against Germany in Munich on 1 September 2001.

The waiting game: Sven-Göran Eriksson and Tord Grip watch the teams warm up before what was to become one of the classic encounters between Germany and England.

Stevie Wonder: Steven Gerrard scores England's second goal to put them 2–1 up against Germany. Michael Owen had levelled things after Germany scored the opener.

Reasons to be cheerful, 1–2–3: Michael Owen is head over heels with delight as he celebrates his hat-trick and David Beckham and Steven Gerrard run to congratulate him.

Crowning glory: Emile Heskey puts his goal (England's fifth) past Oliver Kahn to complete a great night for England.

Unforgettable: The clock counts down to the end of the match and the scoreboard at the Olympiastadion in Munich confirms an amazing result for England.

Carry on scoring: Michael Owen adds to his international tally by scoring the first goal against Albania at St James's Park in Newcastle-upon-Tyne.

Make it two: Robbie Fowler added a second goal for England in the match against Albania to take them to the brink of qualification. Japan and South Korea were one match away.

Give me goals: Sven-Göran Eriksson signals the score between Germany and Finland to the England players, indicating that England needed a draw with Greece in order to qualify.

Spurred on: Teddy Sheringham runs to the fans to celebrate after scoring the first goal against Greece, which brought England back into contention in the match.

Jumping for joy: An understandably ecstatic David Beckham shows his delight after scoring the equaliser for England against Greece from one of his trademark free kicks.

'We're on our way to Wem... er... Japan': The Land of the Rising Sun awaits as the England squad and staff enjoy the celebrations after the match against Greece which finished 2–2.

Guiding light: Sven-Göran Eriksson acknowledges the roar of the fans at Old Trafford and shows his own joy at England's success in qualifying for the FIFA World Cup 2002.

England United: After an emotionally draining match the England team make a tour of the pitch at Old Trafford to thank the fans for their support.

Hard task: Brazilian legend Pele hands FIFA's Michel Zen-Ruffinen the ball containing England's name which sent them into Group F with Argentina, Nigeria and Sweden.

See you in June: Sven-Göran Eriksson shakes hands with the head coach of Nigeria, Amodu Shaibo, after the draw for the finals of the FIFA World Cup which took place in Korea.

Eriksson:

Lazio's captain had to be a symbol for the team. He could have been one of the natural leaders, but not necessarily. You don't normally select a new player to be captain, as he won't know the players, the club, the environment.

What was your personal relationship with the players like?

Eriksson:

I wasn't their mate. I didn't go out and eat with individual players. I wanted to be more like a big brother to them, so that they would come to me if they had problems.

> 'I wanted to be a big brother to the players'

Was this a natural distance?

Eriksson:

Yes, at any rate in Italy. Perhaps I talked too little with the players, and could have taken the initiative more often, in this respect. The easiest time to make contact with the players was after the training sessions, when they looked forward to hearing my comments and ideas. But if they needed to talk, the players also tended to prefer going to the assistant coach or the physio, or someone else who didn't bear the responsibility for the selection of the team.

Even if they didn't talk directly to me, they hoped the message would reach me.

How important was this distance?

Eriksson:

It depends on the culture of the country you're working in. It's like role-play. I wasn't afraid of losing control, it wasn't about that. For example, I tried to discuss team selection with the players in Italy, as I had done in Sweden. It didn't work. Quite simply, they didn't want to have the responsibility for decisions of that nature. The coach had to bear all the responsibility. If things went well, fine – if not, I got fired. Perhaps you could sit down with a core of two or three players and discuss the team.

How did you maintain the motivation of players who had to sit on the bench a lot, or who were injured for a long time?

Eriksson:

The problem was not that they often sat on the bench. They accepted that they were reserves. It was worse with players who were left on the bench only now and again, as they then saw themselves as not up to scratch.

In today's football, with 60 matches per year, you really need two complete teams. So the regular players also have to sit on the bench now and then. Some hang their heads, while others go on the attack and want to show what they're really made of when they get the chance to play again.

It's important to encourage players in this situation, and talk to them more than usual.

How do you see the relationship with the outside world? I'm thinking particularly about the mass media.

Eriksson:

It was difficult to be a player, and for that matter a coach, in Rome.

There were so many supporters, so many commentators, so many opinions among the media, so many people who thought they were the experts. That made it difficult to keep your tactics secret, for example. What you were thinking to yourself was in the papers the next day. Generally speaking, the mass media played too big a role, especially where the players were concerned. If a player was sensitive to criticism in the media, he had to try to change the situation himself. A coach couldn't do it. Players had to try to learn how to live with the pressure caused by constant media attention.

How did you yourself react to the media?

Eriksson:

I was sensitive to it when I began my coaching career in Sweden, but now it takes a lot to make me pay any attention. Nowadays, I'm much more focused on what I'm doing. I mostly listen to colleagues involved with the team, and of course the players.

> 'I pay little attention to the media'

What do the players think about the fact that you are so calm?

Eriksson:

I hope some of it rubs off on the team. The players see that I am active in other ways, of course: making decisions, changes, talking before and after our matches.

You said earlier that individual players had to defer to the squad. Aren't they then in danger of effacing their own personalities?

Eriksson:

As a coach I have changed my outlook on that point. I used to be hard as nails on tactical discipline. Now I go along with the 'discipline with freedom' line. The best players, in particular, can't be put in a straitjacket or they won't be free to use their ability. If I force a player to carry out a task in a certain way, he'll be playing under compulsion instead of with complete freedom. You can generally say that the longer you have a team, the greater freedom you can allow them. If I had been a strict disciplinarian with Mancini, he would have been a poor player. He could find solutions on the field which you wouldn't find in any textbook.

Discipline – but with freedom

Railo:

As we said before, how well a sportsman does will depend on that inner feeling of freedom. But so far as playing systems or tactics are concerned, this doesn't have to conflict with discipline. My experience has been that it's important to have fixed limits, with plenty of freedom between them. The player who goes beyond these limits will certainly feel free himself but is liable to compromise his team-mates. Hard discipline should be instilled where playing systems are concerned, but it should be done with a certain degree of freedom.

How do you deal with the balance between freedom and discipline?

Eriksson:

I try very hard to 'read' the different personalities in a team so that everyone will have their individual needs satisfied – in the context of the team, of course. You can't expect people to act according to the same behavioural patterns all the time. It's important for there to be an individual phase, such as personal training after collective training sessions.

You can also excuse certain players from certain aspects of the squad's training sessions, as long as their team-mates don't get the negative impression that they are being singled out for special treatment.

What are your views on discipline off the pitch?

Eriksson:

I try to be strict where the players' general behaviour towards referees, team-mates and opponents is concerned, and there are consequences if they break the rules we have agreed on. Where their behaviour off the field is concerned, I have set up a small number of rules, but I'm strict about them. Punctuality is important. Players who are not punctual spoil it for the rest of the team, and there's no excuse for that. I'm also hard on alcohol and partying. During my first year at IFK Gothenburg we were regarded as a rebellious bunch and we suffered from players being booked and sent off.

> *Punctuality is very important*

But we overcame that by hard work and, in the end, our behaviour was impeccable, both on and off the field. The team travelled a lot in the Pools Cup (*Tipscupen*) due to the club's finances, but we also used the trips to build a winning culture. Nobody moaned about waiting times, depressing airports or grotty hotel rooms.

Railo:

We know that people react differently, especially when they are under stress. One will want to talk a lot, someone else will be quiet, a picture of concentration. The second guy will then be annoyed that the first guy keeps on talking, while this guy will feel depressed about the lack of company.

Eriksson:

I know what you mean. I try to provide individual solutions where possible. Players are given several hours when they can do what they like – go to a film, or something like that. They can also choose their room-mates themselves. You can't expect everyone to be alike.

> *Treat players as individuals*

How are the players affected by their social environment away from the team?

Eriksson:

Players' performances on the pitch are closely connected to their lives at home. If they are socially insecure, it's going to be reflected in their game. Moving can also be difficult, especially if you're from another country. Clubs should provide more than just a place to live – why not a language course for the whole family so that they can come to grips with the new environment? In situations like this, it's the wives and girlfriends, especially those who have children, who are often the ones up against it. It can be so easy for them to feel isolated.

> The home environment plays an important part

They say that you should never change a winning team. What do you think?

Eriksson:

That's not what I think. I would say instead: always change a winning team. As I pointed out earlier in the book, it can be right to change players if you feel they're not going to find the requisite mental energy. This might seem a bit dramatic, but I think you always have to think about making changes. It doesn't mean that you have to expose the team to a revolution.

> Always change a winning team!

Can you disclose your philosophy of football? What are your ten most important principles?

Eriksson:

My philosophy would look like this:

- Play offensively (mentally and physically).
- Quick passing.
- Think ahead.
- Plenty of running off the ball.
- Close all gaps.
- Organise the team and team management.
- Be positive.
- Stick up for your team.
- Be loyal.
- Accept that people are different.

How would you change your work in future?

Eriksson:

I would want to introduce a leadership philosophy and build a team with a certain style. Whoever didn't fit in would have to go. I would like to build for the long term. Most teams are in too much of a hurry nowadays: they have to win at all costs.

I want to be more of a manager than a coach. I'd prefer to be sitting in the stands with a walkie-talkie, watching the matches. It's easier to see the game from that perspective, make the right decisions, the right changes, give advice to the assistant coaches. Football will be increasingly specialised and will require more expertise than we have today.

Remember:

- Winning cultures can be created.
- Winning cultures develop when the thinking in a group is right.
- It's important to feel proud when you put on the team shirt.
- A culture is built through reward and punishment.
- The individual quickly adapts to the norms of the group.
- Negative thoughts spread more quickly than positive ones.
- Björn Borg was a good example who caught the popular imagination – many others didn't.
- Winning cultures are built by the active promotion of 'good examples' and 'active management'.
- The good team must have a common vision, goal and collective spirit.
- A coach must be sensitive to the balance between personal closeness and distance.
- It is important to have a small number of rules that are strictly applied.
- A good coach is not a yes-man. But neither is he a no-man.
- Always change a winning team.
- Develop your own team philosophy.
- Stick up for your team.
- Accept that people have different needs.
- Play offensively (mentally and physically).
- Think ahead all the time.

MENTAL TRAINING

– *Changing negative to positive*

I move into the penalty area and my position's good, but the goalkeeper is also well placed and their right-back is closing in on me. I see one of my team-mates out of the corner of my eye, but he's under pressure. My brain has a question: shoot or pass? I choose to pass to my team-mate, but he's under such pressure that he finds it difficult to do anything effective.

> 'shall I shoot or pass?'

Afterwards I look at the video and see that the only right thing would have been to shoot, and not pass. But I had a mental block and hesitated.

Mental blocks are very common

Eriksson:

I've seen players with mental blocks in crucial situations thousands of times. What is it that actually happens?

Railo:

There can be a number of explanations. The level of mental tension may be too high, causing a block. Players may respond with flight behaviour or suffer from low self-confidence. Acquired blocks from similar situations on other occasions can also affect a player. We can remove all of these barriers with mental training.

In the case of the player who passed instead of shot, the block had been acquired. The player had missed in similar situations before, so he connected the situation with anxiety and poor technique. His brain had learnt that the situation was difficult and related it to anxiety.

When a block like this takes hold of a player, it is quickly confirmed and reinforced in that the player focuses his thoughts on the problem:

'This is going to be difficult.'

'What if I don't succeed?'

'This is so typical of me.'

'Now I mustn't miss.'

This kind of acquired block can be long-lasting and develop into a negative spiral, both intellectually and emotionally.

> *'This is going to be difficult'*

Eriksson:

Can a thought directly affect our emotions?

Railo:

Yes, our thoughts govern our feelings and mental images, which then affect our performance. As a result, many sportsmen even 'think onto themselves' unnecessary problems – and barriers that hinder development. On the other hand, we can make the negative positive through mental training and fresh thinking. Handled in the right way, a new outlook can clear up established problems and create a new beginning.

Learn tactics and technique faster with mental training

Eriksson:

What actually is mental training?

Railo:

Mental training is simply the automation of positive thoughts, feelings and mental images connected to specific situations. It means that we give the brain new, positive mental programmes.

We use thought to re-learn something which previously had been learnt negatively, so that it becomes positive and problem-free.

> *Make positive thoughts and feelings automatic*

Eriksson:

What you've just said then is that we can actually correct a negative feeling in a situation so that it becomes something positive. I've seen you do this in practice, too. Can we therefore use thought and this type of mental training to control our technique, as well as different situations in football?

Railo:

This is definitely possible. You see, the brain can be said to have a marked 'weakness'. It finds it difficult to differentiate between what you have actually experienced and what you have only thought. It seems to register and store things in the same way. It is this weakness that gives us the unique opportunity to train ourselves mentally.

The brain is truly a remarkable organ in this respect. It stores our thoughts and feelings, governs our reactions and our bodies both consciously and subconsciously. In addition, research and practical experience both show that the brain learns regardless of our surroundings.

> *The brain learns regardless of where we might be*

As a result, we can train technique and tactics by producing inner mental images of good technical and tactical solutions. We can simply sit at home on the sofa, close our eyes and think through the technical and tactical solutions which will reinforce and hasten our practical schooling out on the field.

The advantage of this mental technique is that we can go through several repetitions in a few minutes, whereas on the football pitch we won't encounter the same situation very often during a match or training.

The best effect is achieved through a combination of practical training and mental training. (The effect is increased if we do exercises under relaxed conditions.)

The many uses of mental training

Eriksson:
What other things can you use mental training for?

Railo:
I have used mental training in barrier-breaking goals to

- Set world records
- Be number one in the league
- Become a professional footballer
- Get into the national team
- Qualify for world championships

I've also used mental training to remove anxiety and blocks, such as:

- Fear of missing
- Fear of certain opponents
- Attitudes of the type: 'The away pitch is poor'; 'Hope we don't meet Manchester United'; 'Brazil are unbeatable'.

A third area is in the correction of self-image and role-perception of the type: 'I'm not as good as him'; 'We belong in division three'; 'We won't have a chance in the cup'; 'We always lose when it matters'.

Let me use the example of a player I have worked with who became one of Europe's finest footballers. I first made an analysis before we started mental training. I asked him to close his eyes, relax and see himself coming up against Kevin Keegan, who was then one of Europe's best players.

After five minutes' concentration, I asked him to tell me the thoughts, feelings and mental images that he had experienced. He said that he had been anxious, and thought defensively. He felt that he hadn't got enough courage for the encounter, and he had the following mental picture: he saw himself as much smaller than Kevin Keegan, even though, physically speaking, he was much bigger.

> *Kevin Keegan grew in stature*

This revealed that his brain was not properly programmed. When the brain is incorrectly programmed in this way, it is impossible to make the most of our ability. Our playing ability will never be maximised until the brain has accepted a new mental picture.

We began mental training to get his brain to accept freely a mental picture where he was just as big, strong and effective as the England striker.

I included all this in personal mental training programmes, which I put on a cassette for him. After a few months of mental training, he got rid of his problem and was able to utilise his ability in top-class European competition.

Another example is that of another European forward who had problems scoring goals, especially in the league. He had developed this mental picture: 'I move into the penalty area and it's me alone with the goalkeeper. For every metre I get nearer to the goal and the goalkeeper, the goal gets smaller and smaller and the goalkeeper gets bigger and bigger. And I shoot wide, or over the bar.'

This is a typical example of how the brain can become badly programmed, preventing the player from making the most of his ability.

Eriksson:

You have taken care of many blocks like this, in different sports. Can you tell us how you go about it?

Railo:

Earlier, I mentioned the effect that our thoughts can have on our lives, both in a positive and a negative direction. What I do with mental training is to change old, negative thinking into new, positive thinking. Mental training is the expulsion of negatively learnt impulses, replacing them with new, positive ones. This is the basis of my methodology.

Eriksson:

I was astonished many years ago when you told me of the effect a person's thoughts could have on his life. Can you explain, as simply as possible, how this works?

Railo:

Let me put it this way: a thought conceived in an atmosphere of security will be accepted by the brain. It then has a positive effect.

Looked at the opposite way: a thought conceived in an atmosphere of insecurity will become a mental block. It will put the brakes on.

Eriksson:

Do you believe that people can think problems onto themselves?

Railo:

Definitely. Do you remember what I said about this in the chapter, 'The Power of the Mind'? Thinking in terms of problems and difficulties develops blocks and limitations.

Eriksson:

Then you believe that people can also 'think onto' themselves opportunities and solutions to problems?

> Replace negatively learnt impulses with new, positive ones

Railo:

The answer is yes, but then we have to work systematically over a slightly longer time. Just consider how we talk to ourselves, which is something that everybody does. This 'inner dialogue' is incredibly important for our performance, since it governs our body.

An experiment has shown this. A group of people are told that they are to do press-ups – as many as they can. Before they start, they must take three minutes to talk to themselves with their eyes closed, according to this pattern:

'My arms are weak.'

'My body feels heavy.'

'I'm in poor shape.'

After three minutes of this type of inner dialogue, I let them do press-ups – and count them. A day later, I have the same group sit down, relax and close their eyes.

Their inner dialogues are now to take the opposite direction:

'My arms are strong.'

'My body feels light.'

'I'm in great shape.'

I have them do press-ups again – and I count them. In all the courses in which I have carried out this exercise, we obtained many more press-ups the second time, than the first. And this was only after a three-minute inner dialogue.

> Inner dialogue is important as it governs our body

Eriksson:

So, by systematically changing our 'inner dialogue', we can improve our ability to perform?

Railo:

That's exactly right. A systematic, positive inner dialogue will gradually drive out the negative dialogue and produce a positive outcome.

Eriksson:

Can you give us more examples of positive and negative inner dialogues?

Railo:

A negative inner dialogue can go like this:

'I'm going to make a mistake again.'

'The others are bigger than me.'

'I never do well against this team.'

'Why is it just me that has bad luck?'

'The away ground is tough.'

A positive inner dialogue can go like this:

'Everybody makes mistakes, it won't bother me.'

'I'll have a go against anybody, regardless of the situation.'

'I'm not bothered about the other guy, I'll do my own thing.'

'Everyone can have bad luck, but I'm going to have a go.'

> *Our subconscious prevents us from performing at our best*

Railo:

A theme throughout the book is how our subconscious prevents us from performing to the best of our ability.

- We are rooted in roles and patterns.
- We think negatively and limit ourselves.
- We are defensive and choose a way out far too often.
- We are governed by the compulsion, instead of the freedom, to perform.
- We have blocks and mental barriers that keep us prisoner in a performance cage.

All this can be changed by mental training. As we have said, mental training is a question of using our mind, concentration and mental images to achieve positive reactions. As a result, we don't have to re-live a situation physically in order to change our reactions. However, breaking through unconscious barriers is a process which can take time.

It's like training a muscle: if we repeat an exercise a sufficient number of times, the muscle will develop and become stronger. If we repeat a thought a sufficient number of times, the brain will develop – and the thought will take root.

> *The mind is like a muscle. It too has to be trained*

This is how we train mentally

Begin with a little self-analysis. Sit down and relax completely, close your eyes and think yourself into a situation that you know has given you problems. While you do this, allow your mind to work quite freely, without any conscious control. The only thing you are to do, is make a note of all the negative thoughts and feelings which arise. Write them down.

The next step is to turn your negative reactions into positive ones.

Try to find desirable reactions: how you would wish to react in the same situations. Write these down too.

Let me show you different ways of thinking and responding in the same situation. Before I begin my training plan, let me tell you about a goalkeeper and a striker and their thinking before and after mental training. The goalkeeper suffered a negative reaction when he let in goals. He felt the pressure from his team-mates and became defensive and fearful.

His negative reactions can be described as follows:

'I'm afraid of the ball.'

'I'm worried about what the others think.'

'I mustn't miss again.'

'I'm getting angry with myself.'

'I can't accept myself.'

'I mustn't miss now'

The goalkeeper practised these reactions through mental training:

'I feel calm.'

'I'm attacking.'

'I accept myself.'

'I dare to go for the ball.'

'I'm not bothered about what the others think.'

The striker had negative feelings and thoughts whenever he had an opponent at his back. His reactions were:

'I feel alarmed.'

'I feel insecure.'

'I feel defensive.'

'I can't accept the responsibility.'

'I lose control.'

'My technique isn't up to much.'

The reactions we worked on mentally were these:

'I feel OK with an opponent at my back.'

'I feel confident and secure with opponents at my back.'

'I feel strong with opponents at my back.'

'I can "see" my technique for dealing with opponents at my back.'

In practice, I set up my method in a training plan. Below I give some examples from footballers I have worked with. As I said, my mental training plan amounts to replacing negative reactions, learnt earlier, by positive ones. This I do by controlling the thinking involved

safe, strong and secure

Mental training plan

THE GOALKEEPER FROM MILAN		
Tough situation	**Undesirable reactions**	**Desirable reactions**
1. Meet tough opponents	Feel small Feel listless Feel insecure Feel passive Feel defensive	Feel big Feel fit Feel secure Feel active Feel attacking
2. I let in goals	Become nervous Get angry with myself Don't accept myself Lose self-confidence Worried about the next shot	Feel calm Talk positively to myself Accept myself Not bothered about what the others think.

THE PLAYER FROM MANCHESTER UNITED		
Tough situation	**Undesirable reactions**	**Desirable reactions**
Shoot with left foot	Feel like I can't The goalkeeper will save it Become nervous	I have the hardest shot I score great goals I strike the ball perfectly The ball flies off my boot I dare

THE FORWARD FROM JUVENTUS		
Tough situation	**Undesirable reactions**	**Desirable reactions**
Score goals Shoot Head	I can't score goals Think I'm going to miss Don't want the ball Don't go to the goal	I see where the goalkeeper's going I see the gaps I want the ball I go straight to the goal I give everything I've got

THE PLAYER FROM LAZIO		
Tough situation	**Undesirable reactions**	**Desirable reactions**
1. Head under pressure	Afraid of being hit Afraid of not heading well I am weak in the air	I am fit I'm tough, my body's hard I go up and win duels
2. Cross Corner Free kick	Afraid it'll be too high The ball goes straight to the goalkeeper Don't want to risk it	I hit beautiful crosses Hard, curving crosses My crosses result in goals I dare

THE PLAYER FROM IFK GOTHENBURG		
Tough situation	**Undesirable reactions**	**Desirable reactions**
1. Don't see the game as a whole	Afraid of not seeing the game Look up too late Don't know where opponents and team-mates are I am stressed Am not following the game	Feel calm Know what's going to happen See the game On top of the game Find creative solutions
2. Give up too soon	Apathetic, immobile Not participating Want to, but not up to fighting	Always take the ball Step on the gas Taking part all the time Daring

THE PLAYER FROM REAL MADRID		
Tough situation	**Undesirable reactions**	**Desirable reactions**
1. Penalties	The goalkeeper takes it I miss We lose I can't score penalties	I'm calm I feel in control I fool the goalkeeper I score a goal
2. The left foot	I kick the ground I shoot and it goes wide I miss – surprise, surprise I'm no good with my left Feel insecure	Passing will be good I can shoot with both feet I'm good with my left I'm secure I score a goal

With mental training, therefore, players first think through one or several difficult situations – then try to connect them to desirable reactions. They have first to sit down and shut their eyes, then after a minute or two, begin to think about the desirable reactions they entered in their analysis earlier. Let this take from three to five minutes. The brain will gradually connect the earlier problem to new, positive reactions – it is quite simply a question of training.

An example with a forward: as soon as he 'felt' that a player came up behind him in his mental training, we inserted the desirable reactions. After a period of training, he was able to create mental images of how he elegantly and cheekily sold his opponent a dummy – and in the end he was able to do it in match situations.

Mental training can take place on two levels:

1. We consciously change our thinking on a daily basis in accordance with the principles described here. This can be done at home on the sofa, on a bus and, not least, out on the training ground.

2. We learn a technique to relax deeply and work positively on our problems in that condition over long periods, normally for between 10 and 15 minutes each time, three or four times a week.

Remember that mental training can be used both to improve technique and tactics and for faster acquisition of these skills. In principle, training proceeds as we have described it above: we create a mental picture of the desired condition – in this case, that we master a particular technique – and mentally train with this. We 'see' that we carry out the technique as we would like to, at the same time forcing out mental pictures of using the technique incorrectly. The point is that the brain has to have clear images that can function as the control for our new behaviour, technically, tactically and mentally.

Pelé, Zidane, Figo and Beckham – fast outer pace but inner calm

When we train mentally, we should set up certain guidelines:

THINK, OUTER PACE – INNER CALM

Football is a fast game, and this leads to a fast inner, mental pace. This in turn results in players in pressured situations not being calm enough to do the right thing. They shoot over the goal, or far wide of it, because of a lack of inner calm and control. Some players manage to keep a very high outer rhythm, and still manage to keep their inner calm in complicated, pressured situations. This gives good technical and mental control and the ability to assess play.

Some sportsmen possess natural ability in this area. In football, names such as Pelé, Zidane, Figo and Beckham come to mind. Meanwhile, most players are confused by the outer pace of the game and make too many mistakes. We saw many examples of this at the 2000 European Championship in France – not least, when Holland were knocked out on penalties.

We must mention the French reserve, Sylvain Wiltord, in the final between Italy and France. With three of the four minutes of injury time gone, he received the ball far out on the left in a pressure situation. The stress on the French players was now great: an Italian title was only 50 seconds away.

Wiltord kept his inner calm and shot with power and precision past Toldo in the Italian goal. Most players would have shot wide from a similar position. Then David Trezeguet hit the winner for France in extra-time.

This example also illustrates, naturally, that among other things we should never give up – an old but enduring truth. Inner calm can be trained through mental training. Food for thought therefore: outer speed – inner calm.

> *'It's fast out there – but inside I'm calm'*

THINK AHEAD – NOT BACK

Generally speaking, it's better to use our concentration to look ahead. In a race, isn't it better to direct our concentration on the runner in front and not on the one behind? If there isn't a runner in front, we can search out points in the terrain or on the track and set our sights on them, producing a feeling that we are being 'sucked' towards these points.

In tennis, we might think about retrieving a weak position or – if we are in the lead – increasing our advantage. The important thing is that our concentration should be directed forward, offensively, and that our inner dialogue runs along the lines of 'Now let's go!' and not 'What will I do if he...?'

THINK OUTWARDS – NOT INWARDS

Many people react to signals from their bodies – tiredness, lactic acid – by becoming completely engrossed with them. Their concentration is directed inwards, towards the body. Experience says that it is better to direct our concentration outwards, away from ourselves. Otherwise, there is a danger that by concentrating on our own tiredness, we will feel even more tired.

THINK OF TECHNIQUE – OR NOT

Where technical sports are concerned, we must train and compete in different ways, at least mentally. When we are training and learning technique, our concentration should be focused on technique. In this way we become conscious of various details more quickly, and establish an emotional connection to the fact that we can handle the technique.

However, in competition we should instead choose to direct our concentration away from technique, which should be so well ingrained that the body should be able to perform it on its own. It's more or less the same when you drive a car: the technique of driving must be second nature to us so that we can concentrate on the traffic outside the car.

> *Learn it and forget it*

An example from bowling: two players were both very good – and very evenly matched. During a break, the experienced bowler went up to his younger opponent and said, 'You use your thumb very cleverly. How do you do that?'

The younger bowler immediately began to wonder just how exactly he did do it. His concentration became directed away from the competition to his technique, his automatic reactions disappeared – and he lost.

DON'T THINK NEGATIVELY

We very often direct our concentration to something that isn't working very well at the time. The sportsman might begin to concentrate on not making mistakes – instead of on doing things right. The difference might sound subtle, but it is crucial.

For example, during a tournament, a golfer began to screw the ball way over to the right. At his next shot, he thought, 'Now I'm not going to hit it to the right!' He promptly hit it even further to the right. There are any number of examples of how concentrating on not making a mistake leads to a repetition of the mistake – again and again.

THINK SIMPLY

Technique which leads to good performance is often difficult. On the other hand, it often leads to our concentration being directed to exactly that – technique. Instead, we should mentally train ourselves to apprehend technique as simply as possible. Once we have trained ourselves, the body's aptitude for automation (see above) is well able to leave us with the notion that technique is simple. How many licensed drivers do we know who think it is difficult to drive a car?

THINK 'THING' – NOT PERSON

We don't play against another person. We oppose another player. Thus, it is another person's performance we have to defeat – not another person.

There is a definite danger that our own performance will suffer if we begin to concentrate too much on our opponent as a person.

Our thoughts should be directed instead to style of play, technique, tactics and strategy, and we should try to marginalise our emotional engagement with our opponent as a person. Think: "I'm not competing against you – I'm competing against your technique!"

THINK IN TERMS OF YOUR OWN CONTROL ROOM

It is crucially important to control, and not be controlled by, the public, the mass media, opponents and situations.

If we let those things become factors in our performance, we will probably do well when everything around us is going well, but worse when it is not. The point here is that we should be our own master, and not be reliant on our situation and environment. We can build our own control room and run it as the tightest of ships – and entirely by ourselves. In our control room we will think as follows:

'In here, I say what goes.'

'I'm the master in my room.'

'I'm strong in my room.'

'I'm secure in my room.'

'I'm not bothered by what my opponent does.'

'I go my own way.'

'I control my own technique.'

Build your own control room

Remember:

- Mental training is about getting the brain to learn faster by controlling our thought processes.
- Mental training gives inner calm even under a fast outer pace.

Mental training can be used to:

- Increase our ability to concentrate.
- Remove blocks due to anxiety.
- Build self-confidence.
- Re-program the brain when it has been poorly programmed.
- Remove stress reactions.
- Increase the effect of rest.
- Break through barriers.
- Acquire technique faster.
- Learn the team's different tactics faster.

CLOSING WORDS

– The beginning of a pilgrimage

Eriksson:

The power of the mind really is incredible.

Railo:

Yes. I don't think it's exaggerating to say, as we somewhat provocatively said at the beginning, that the psychological difference is decisive in today's sport and determines who is going to be number one, and who second, third, fourth. When everybody has trained to the limit, competitions and matches are decided by whoever best utilises his resources – and this in turn is often decided by how the mind governs in different situations.

Eriksson:

Of course, everybody doesn't compete at the top level and have the chance of winning the World Cup or the Italian League.

Railo:

That's true. But everybody can use mental training. Joggers, too, can set up barrier-breaking goals and mentally train to achieve them – in exactly the same way as a top sportsman. We all have a unique upper mental limit which prevents us from accessing all our resources. And I'm not only talking about sport. For example, there is a danger that we get stuck in a performance cage in our jobs, too, that we don't dare to do something for fear of failing, that we are paralysed by performance anxiety.

It's fairly easy to take the examples in sport that we have used and apply them to our working lives. We can also create mental pictures of how we manage a particular situation – then mentally work with these images.

Many people feel cowed – just to take one example – by the thought of speaking in front of a large group of people. In this case, we can create a mental picture of the situation and connect it to positive feelings. There's no limit to the number of uses that mental training can have.

Remember that there are no quick, easy solutions. Everything takes time. Everything must be given the time it needs. Changing our way of thinking is a process that can tax our patience – but at the same time, it can be the basis of our development.

Start to think now about the challenges that you have taken on in the last few years, whether you react with fight or flight to changes in your life, whether you have an offensive inner dialogue – or a defensive one.

We'll conclude with a Japanese proverb: 'A problem is a mountain filled with treasure.' Both mountains and problems can be daunting and difficult to overcome, but we can also find much on the way that is enlightening and rewarding.

And who said that in sport, or in life, our pilgrimage was going to be an easy one?

The publishers would like to thank the following sources for their kind permission to reproduce the pictures in this book:

Plate section one:

Allsport UK Ltd/Grazia Neri 1t

Action Images/Michael Regan 8b John Sibley 1b, Darren Walsh 5t, 5b, 6t, 7

FAOPL 2t, 2b, 3t, 3b, 4tl, 4tr, 4b, 6b, 8t

Plate section two:

Allsport UK Ltd/Shaun Botterill 8b, 8t,

Action Images 6t/Richard Heathcote 1b, 2b , Michael Regan 4b, John Sibley 2t, 3t, 5b, 7t, Darren Walsh 6b

Empics/Neal simpson 5t

FAOPL 1t, 3b, 4t, 7b

Every effort has been made to acknowledge correctly and contact the source and/or copyright holder of each picture, and Carlton Books Limited apologises for any unintentional errors or omissions which will be corrected in future editions of this book.